Henry Carr Glyn Moule

Thoughts on the Spiritual Life

Henry Carr Glyn Moule

Thoughts on the Spiritual Life

ISBN/EAN: 9783337336790

Printed in Europe, USA, Canada, Australia, Japan

Cover: Foto ©Lupo / pixelio.de

More available books at **www.hansebooks.com**

Thoughts

ON

The Spiritual Life

BY

H. C. G. MOULE, M.A.

Principal of RIDLEY HALL, *and late Fellow of* TRINITY COLLEGE, CAMBRIDGE

Author of "THOUGHTS ON CHRISTIAN SANCTITY," "THOUGHTS ON UNION WITH CHRIST," *&c.*

"I live by the faith of the Son of God, who loved me, and gave Himself for me."—GAL. ii. 20.

THIRTEENTH THOUSAND.

LONDON

SEELEY & CO., ESSEX STREET, STRAND.

1889

LONDON:
WOODFALL AND KINDER, PRINTERS,
70 TO 76, LONG ACRE, W.C.

CONTENTS

I. PAGE

Work and Faith 9

II.

The Total Abstinence of the Gospel 26

III.

Christian Moderation. . . . 44

IV.

The Will of God 58

V.

Pleasure in Infirmities . . . 73

VI.

Conflict and Peace 86

VII. PAGE

Manifoldness 108

VIII.

Grace for Grace 122

IX.

Living Water 134

X.

Christian Service 149

XI.

Concluding Thoughts 166

XII.

Hymns 180

PREFATORY NOTE

THE following chapters have been written as a sequel, in some sort, to two little volumes already published, "Thoughts on Christian Sanctity," and "Thoughts on Union with Christ." The writer here takes for granted much which has been spoken of in detail there. On the other hand, as this book may of course fall into the hands of readers who have not seen those, no over-careful effort has been made to avoid re-statements altogether.

In most cases the chapters are headed by words of Holy Scripture. Throughout the book the author has sought to keep in constant view the promises, cautions, and precepts of the written Word, as the one sure basis and final appeal in all things concerning the source and action of the regenerate life. Every year brings its fresh witness to the need of a watchful, loving, and most reverent loyalty to the Holy Scriptures, for all who would not drift they know not where from "the hope set before us."

In writing, the author has had much in his heart and thoughts the spiritual needs of those engaged in more or less direct work for the kingdom of our Lord.

Earnestly does he request the prayers of his readers, whatever be their convictions on the subjects here treated. He asks for the prayer that the Lord Jesus Christ, the Master, may in some way be magnified in these pages, and that His bond-servant may know better and better the blessedness of living by Him and for Him alone. To Him, speaking in His Word, what is written is wholly submitted.

RIDLEY HALL, CAMBRIDGE,
St Luke's Eve, Oct. 17, 1887.

I.

WORK AND FAITH.

Gal. ii. 20.—The life which I live in the flesh I live by the faith of (*i.e.*, by faith in) the Son of God, who loved me and gave Himself for me.

Joh. vi. 29.—This is the work of God, that ye believe on Him whom He hath sent.

We are about to engage in some thoughts
on the principles and practice of the
Spiritual Life. That Life, as to its source
and secret, is "in the Son of God," 1 Joh. v. 11.
the Gift of the Father; in Him who is
"the Life," as well as "the Way and the Joh. xiv. 6.
Truth." As to its reception, it is received in receiving Him; "he that hath 1 Joh. v. 12.
the Son hath the life." As to its issue,

exercise, and manifestation, it is the doing
of the Will of God in all things, with a
chastened, penitent, peaceful and loving
confidence in Him as He is revealed and
reconciled in Jesus Christ our Lord. As
to its standard, it recognizes nothing lower
1 Joh. iii. than His revealed holiness; "even as He
3. is pure." As to its purpose and hope,
it looks, with a faith reposed upon His
1 Thess. promise and power, to "walk pleasing
iv. 1. Him;" here and now, under the shelter
of the atoning Cross, and hereafter to
1 Joh. iii. be indeed "like Him, seeing Him as
2. He is."

As to its beginning and its maintenance, both of them are, from the divine side, by the Holy Spirit, "the Lord, the Giver of Life," who brings Christ and the soul together. From the side of human experience, both of them are by faith, by submissive reliance on the promise and the Promiser. Faith is the hand that accepts the bread and the water of Life, the mouth that eats and that drinks them. From first to last the Life of God, like the Righteousness of God, "is revealed from faith to faith." Rom. i. 17.

First among our detailed thoughts upon this sacred Life I place now this—an enquiry into the place of Spiritual Effort in a life which is as yet in its essence everywhere and always a walk by faith, a life of faith. There is such a place. Work (I speak here of the spiritual and internal kind of work) not only has a function beside that of the happy quietism of a God-given reliance on the Lord and reception out of His fulness; it has a deep relation to it and connexion with it.

This connexion is not always recognized in Christian thought and exposition. Things are sometimes said about the life of holy faith, the life of rest upon and in the Son of God, which leave, or

seem to leave, no place for spiritual effort
and resolve. Yet the Scriptures have
very much to say about these latter things.
1 Pet. i. 13. They speak of "girding up the loins of
Phil. ii. 12. the mind," of "working out salvation,"
Heb. iv. 11. of "being in earnest" (our English Bible
renders it "labouring") "to enter into
2 Pet. i. 10. the" heavenly "rest," of "giving diligence to make our calling and election
1 Thess. v. 6. sure," of "watching and being sober," of
1 Cor. ix. 27. "keeping under the body and bringing it
Col. iv. 12. into subjection," of "labouring fervently
in prayer." We may be very sure, then, that this fact of spiritual effort is no accident of the Spiritual Life, but a large and vital truth in it. It would be strange if it were otherwise. All conscious personal life has much to do with exercise and effort in the course of its healthful development. A life, conscious and personal, which should be a life of mere and pure quiescence, would hardly

be a life worth living. Could we wish for such a condition of the Spiritual Life?

In the passages quoted at the head of this chapter we find some divine suggestions of the true connexion between the repose of faith and resolute spiritual exertion.

i. In the words to the Galatians St Paul puts before us, from his own experience, that delightful truth, dear to saints of all times and very specially called to remembrance in our own—the truth that the believer's life "in the flesh," amidst concrete conditions and surroundings in a fallen world, is to be continuously lived by faith. He is to "act, and grow, and thrive," to deny self, and bear the cross, and bring forth fruit, by faith; by repose and reliance on his Lord and Head, by a perpetual turning to, and looking to, and receiving from, the Lord Jesus Christ, in all the fulness, and glory, and beauty, of His Person and Work.

The divine method of spiritual victory and service lies in this, that our life is by faith, by submissive trust.

By submissive trust we entered, at our spiritual new birth, at our true coming to Christ, beneath the blessed covert of Justification; and there we abide and remain, never to venture from beneath it for one moment to the end; never to step out on to the forbidden and fatal ground of acceptance for our works' sake, for our state's sake.

And now meantime, by the same way, by submissive trust, we who dwell beneath that covert are to gather up there *this* great treasure of power and peace. He who is our justifying and imputed Righteousness is also, by His Spirit, our sanctifying and inherent Life; and it is faith, mere and simple faith, submissive trust, that receives and feeds on Him as such. To His life and victory, to His holy fulness, we unite ourselves by faith, and by faith only. When temptation comes, our method is to fall back upon and to stand in our King who has conquered for us; to join ourselves, we may say, to His victory; to act upon the fact that we are joined to Him who has overcome, who is the Overcomer. So trusting, so living, His victory is for me, is mine, is as it were conveyed to His member, to me.

Here is our answer, for example, to the problem and torture of vain and evil thoughts, that stir as if uncontrollable in the mind. What are we to do? We entrust ourselves to the Son of God, who by His Spirit, by the Holy Comforter, dwells in us and we in Him. By implicit trust we unite our weary selves, in a special sense for the special need, to Him who in His impeccable and now glorified Manhood has won the victory over every form of evil, for us His members, His body. Again and again let us press home that truth upon our souls. Let nothing becloud it for us. Let no discussion over its details, nay, let no distortions, exaggerations, or parodies of it, make us doubt the thing itself, or forget to use it. The life of peace, of patience, of simplicity, of purity, of hope, of love—the holy life—it is the gift, the ever present gift, of God; and it is given through faith in His blessed Son.

Not long ago I met with a passage to this purpose in the life of that truly great Christian, Dr Thomas Chalmers; a man who certainly was no visionary, no dreamer. It occurs in his diary, of the year 1813 (*Memoir*, vol. i. p. 327):—"Was fatigued by exertion, and instead of following after God by hard straining of the mind, I gave myself to quietism, and feel that looking up for the Spirit through Jesus Christ is the only effectual attitude for obtaining love to God and filial confidence in Him." *

Blessed is the reality of which Chalmers here speaks. Good and fruitful it is to look for life, love, and power altogether away from the processes and resources of self, to that fulness of the Spirit which dwells in Christ for us. Writer and reader, let us unite in making daily proof of this.

ii. But where then is the place for effort? Such a place there is, as we have seen, amply recognized in the Word of God, and never to be discredited in our teaching or thinking. Perhaps the word "effort" is not the best; let us rather

* I observe the following entry three days later, March 24, 1813:—"Began 'Marshall on Sanctification,' and promise myself great enlargement and solidity from this performance." Marshall's "Gospel Mystery of Sanctification" is not light reading, but (shall I say *for*?) it is a book of goid

say "work." In the case of the body it is, I believe, a medical maxim that what wears and kills is not work, but effort; fitful, acute, abnormal exertion. And the word "work" is sanctioned by our blessed Lord Himself, in the passage quoted at the head of this chapter; Joh. vi. 29.

What sort of work is indicated there by the divine Teacher? It is the work, the labour, involved in getting to know, and to remember, what and why to believe. It is the mental and spiritual work of inquiry, judgment, recollection, applied to the subject of Jesus Christ, with a view to trust. This, I am persuaded, is the bearing of our Lord's words at Capernaum. But even should the reader think otherwise about that passage, the truth which to my mind those words convey is a truth conveyed by many another Scripture. It is delightfully implied, for example, in the words of St Paul quoted also above: "The Son of God, who loved me, and gave Himself for me." For that brief claus eis encugh to shew us the Apostle at work in the way of memory, and judgment, and estimate, and contemplation; gathering up the facts of his Lord's Person and Work, and of his own relations to his Lord in consequence. And all this is working, working upon the grounds of faith. Every deliberate process of recollection is internal work; every habit of thought so developed is developed by work. The Christian believer works when he takes earnest pains and uses proper means to gather and to keep together within him the revealed facts about Jesus Christ and life in Him. He works when he dwells in soul on Who He is, on what He has done, and is doing now; on the mystery of His Natures, on the glory of His Person, on His Atonement,

His Exaltation, His Headship, His royal High Priesthood, His Intercession; on the revealed privileges and resources of Union with Him. He works, too, when he deliberately and diligently bears in mind his own perpetual needs, of sinfulness and weakness. All this is work, internal work, not to be done automatically, or as in a dream; not to be done by "trusting it to be done." And great is the need of such work, more than ever great, if possible, in an age like ours, at once so occupied and, alas, so superficial.

The word "recollectedness" was a favourite word with our Christian forefathers, in the vocabulary of spiritual life. It conveyed well the thought of a deliberately formed, and steadily maintained, acquaintance with our deep need in ourselves and our spiritual riches in our Lord, and the temper of mind in which those riches could best be applied to the needs of life.

But recollectedness, if it implies such things, cannot be found and kept without care, thought, resolve; without time saved or made; without persevering acts and habits. In order that we may live indeed by faith on the Son of God, we must, as to the rule and usage of our lives, set apart time, at whatever sacrifice, to ascertain and weigh what are those great treasures on which we are to draw. We must make prayer a real work; we must dig with real toil into our inexhaustible Bible, reverently, painstakingly, and with method; we must cultivate habits of *worship*, public and private—by many Christians too much neglected; we must use the divinely appointed ordinances of the Church of God.

Nor must we vainly think, as too many allow themselves to do, that we have "risen above" articulate doctrines, and may spare ourselves mental pains about

them; a thought which leaves many a pious but indolent mind exposed in a very helpless way to the spell of *false* doctrines, well and sympathetically stated. "In
1 Cor. xiv. 20. understanding we must be men"; and that means a development not attainable without exercise.

iii. Such work, and this is my main point in the present chapter, is right, and rightly directed, when it protects and guides the exercise of faith. On the other hand, and this must be reiterated with most earnest emphasis, such work is not identical with faith; it has not the function of faith; it cannot for one moment take the place of faith. Within the protective circle of such diligence faith is to live and act in its divine simplicity; submissive trust in the Son of God, personal reliance upon and reception from Him whose Person and Work we thus diligently hold in holy "recollection." Not work but trust is our organ, so to speak, for contact with Him, whether as to His righteousness for our acceptance, or as to His Spirit for our power. Yes, faith, in its simplest definition; that faith of which almost every miracle in the Gospels supplies a practical description. Faith, in the view of Jesus Christ, is personal trust. It is no mere condition which entitles us to touch Him. It is itself the touch. Not by toil of thought and will, but by that simplest touch, do I receive the Spirit of the Lord, the life and power of the Head. Toil of thought and will has a large work to do, as we have seen. But faith, and only faith, is the magnetic contact, if we may call it so, with Him. Such is His revealed order.

Let us rest, therefore. Let us labour, therefore. The life of faith in Jesus Christ is indeed a life of liberty, but not an easy-going life. Ease, indeed, there is in it, a sacred ease of certainty, of an acceptance we have not precariously won, but possess in Christ; a sense of wealth at our disposal, of power not our own, power far greater than the enemy's, and exercised on a vantage-ground; but nothing casual and careless. There must be spiritual work that there may be a steady use of spiritual faith.

I would not be mistaken, as if I thought nothing of the most momentary and unprepared glance of the hard-pressed soul on Him who is our Peace and Victory. But I am speaking of the normal, habitual aspects of daily Christian life. If in that life, as to its wont and habit, we would know our Master's power, we dare not leave faith to be exercised anyhow, so to speak. We must recollect, in order to believe, with a deliberate and watchful
2 Pet. iii. 18. recollection. We must "grow in the knowledge of our Lord and Saviour."

"I know whom I have believed, and am persuaded that He is able to keep that which I have committed to Him, against that day." The Apostle "believed"; he had "committed" a great "deposit" to Him in whom his faith rested. And the exercise of that blessed personal confidence—how much it had to do, alike in its rise and its progress, with knowledge of the glorious Person in question, with thought upon His fulness of grace and truth, and with inference, strong and deep, as to the divine results of trust! 2 Tim. i. 12.

Lord, make us by Thy Spirit every day so to work as to believe with ever simpler faith; so to recollect as to rest indeed in Thee. Amen.

II.

THE TOTAL ABSTINENCE OF THE GOSPEL.

Eph. iv. 1, 2, 31.—I, therefore, the prisoner of the Lord, beseech you that ye walk worthy of the vocation wherewith ye are called, with all lowliness and meekness, with longsuffering, forbearing one another in love . . . Let all bitterness, and wrath, and anger, and clamour, and evil-speaking, be put away from you, with all malice.

At the opening of the previous chapter we recollected in passing, among the facts of the Spiritual Life, the spotless purity of the rule and standard of its exercise. Some reflections on this may fitly follow at once on what we have seen of the way of reception of its power, and the self-discipline that must surround such reception. Our

view shall be a very simple and practical one. Behind it all, above it all, shall be remembered that word of the Apostle, "even as He is pure." But we will look 1 Joh. iii. 3.
for application at some of the plainest and homeliest regions of Christian practice.

The connexion of the third chapter of the Ephesians with the fourth is in itself a deep and precious spiritual lesson. Up to the end of the third chapter the Apostle has been led from height to height, from strength to strength, of the heavenly truth. The way of the salvation of the saints, in that plan of God which stretches from eternity to eternity, has been his theme. The Father's choice, the blood of the Son, the work of the regenerating and enlightening Holy Spirit; union with Christ; the indwelling of Christ by the Spirit in the heart; knowledge of the love which passes knowledge;

a filling with the fulness of God ; contact with a power able to do more than prayer or thought attains ; such have been the topics. Now, in the fourth chapter, begins the application of these wonderful principles and resources ; and what is it to be? Out of such a rock what mighty flood of overwhelming energy and action is to rush? We look, and lo there is no rush, no commotion ; in some respects there is little action. The stream is deep, but still and quiet; as, indeed, it well may be, for its element is life eternal, and eternity is calm. The most immediate, and important, and characteristic result of the full truth and power of the Gospel, of the revealed glories of the believer's part and life in Christ, is, according to St Paul, lowliness, meekness, longsuffering, forbearance in love ; a cessation of bitterness, and wrath, and clamour, and unkind words. Sacred paradox of the

Gospel! The Gospel is a motive power strong beyond all others; but it works in the quiet of the soul, in that living quiet caused and secured by the believer's discovery of the wonder of his pardon, and of his safety, and of his privilege; of his union with his Lord, of his Lord's work finished for him, and his Lord's presence abiding in him. Thus the Christian's life is primarily a life of blessed submission, abstinence, and cessation, as the basis of all its action in and for the Lord. Its essential spirit is the very opposite to all ideas of self-assertion, noise and bluster about itself, heraldry of its gifts and graces, comparison of one's own discoveries, attainments, powers and triumphs, with those of others, to their disadvantage. He in whose heart Christ dwelleth, and into whom the fulness of God floweth, must be known, amongst other marks, by "esteeming others better than himself," Phil. ii. 3.

unaffectedly and cordially. In him self has been dethroned as towards God, by sovereign grace; it must be dethroned by the same power as towards men. And this must come out in the practical form of a meek and quiet spirit, pervading all his life.

Such is the general complexion of this delightful passage. And now one leading and most important detail in it is the absoluteness, the totality, which marks its gracious precepts. I venture, in view of this, to entitle this chapter "The Total Abstinence of the Gospel"; total abstinence from allowed sinning, and particularly now from sinning against the law of lowliness, meekness, patience, and kindness, in word, work, and will. The words Total Abstinence have a familiar reference to one form of philanthropic effort in face of a great and terrible need. But I do not speak of this here. I claim the phrase for this yet greater and nobler application, in the light of the word of God. I use it, for myself and for my reader, in regard not of strong drink but of allowed sin. Total Abstinence from *this* is the very watchword of the true Christian's daily rule.

It has sometimes been said that we, who firmly believe in the Christian's need to the very last to confess himself a sinner, to confess his sins, are guilty of "allowing a little sin." God forbid that such a thing should be *truly* said of our principle, and purpose, and aim in the presence of the Lord. It is one thing to hold, in the light of Scripture, and in view of experience, that to the last here below our reception of perfect grace is imperfect; that to the last the light of God has enough to shew us about ourselves to humble us in the dust, now, before Him; that there is sin, and more sin than we

can tell, even in one imperfectly reverent thought of HIM; to say nothing of cruder forms of ill. It is another thing to "allow a little sin," even the least; to think it a trifle to lose a moment's patience, to live half an hour's selfishness, to speak one unkind sentence, or use one unfair argument, to entertain one envious or repining thought, to wander in wish and fancy while we worship, to neglect plain, simple duties (perhaps) in favour of spiritual luxuries. To "allow" such things is grievous sin. To say that anything whatever that is not in the mathematically straight line of God's will does not matter, that it is an unimportant detail, that we cannot
Jer. vii. 10. help it, that "we are delivered to do it";
this indeed is sin. Not one of these things
1 Thess. v. 18. "is the will of God in Jesus Christ concerning us." Not one of these things, as we look back upon it, need have taken place. Against them, each and all, lay the rule of

spiritual Total Abstinence; and grace was ours in Christ Jesus, for each moment as it came.

Such is the holy burthen of this Ephesian passage. The highly privileged and endowed Christian is to walk with ALL lowliness, and to put aside ALL bitterness.

True to its divine practicality, the Gospel here presses home its Total Abstinence just where we might be tempted most easily to forget it. It does not speak of "some great thing." It says nothing about a total abstinence from murmuring when some great desolation falls upon life, or from resentment when some unusual and phenomenal wrong is inflicted on property or person. It speaks of the little things of the common day, the present day. It touches on our feelings and temper this hour about other people, and the outcome of those feelings in the tiny things which in their millions make up

life. The Apostle makes the humiliating and instructive, yet loving, assumption that these supremely privileged believers will yet need, amongst themselves, to
See also Col. iii. 12–15. "bear and forbear"; and he calls upon them, each for himself, ALWAYS to do so. He draws up for them a very practical, a very plain, prosaic, unimaginative list of sins and their opposite graces; and in these matters, not in things heroic, he calls for a Total Abstinence.

Let me deviate for a moment, in illustration, to St John. In his First Epistle
1 Joh. iii. 16, 17. we read two verses side by side. One bids us to stand ready to lay down our lives for the brethren; the other warns us not to shut up our pity from a brother or sister destitute of daily food, if we say we have the love of God in us. The collocation of the verses is significant. A certain poetic glamour surrounds, in imagination, a self-sacrificing dying hour;

we think the occasion itself, perhaps, would sustain us by its greatness. But is there no risk of being caught in the very midst of such imaginations by some small trial of our temper, some unwelcome call upon our time and trouble, and of being fairly conquered by this trial, because unready? Now St John means that this is altogether wrong. The two things are of a piece. If we would be really ready for a self-sacrificing death we must be ready for the next humble little action of a self-sacrificing life, in Jesus Christ, in the Holy Spirit, totally abstaining from its opposite.

To return to St Paul. In his divinely-guided list here of occasions for Total Abstinence, he touches many a point, so it seems to me, which very often proves a weak point in those who really know and love Jesus Christ, and have sincerely surrendered their life and self to Him, and are whole-heartedly on His side, in a deep, true sense, and energetic in His work. Sins are named or implied in this passage which even in inmost circles of Christian life and intercourse are all too often to be seen and mourned.

Is there no such thing as "evil speaking" in the form of religious gossip; the willing, easy, worse than useless, talking over of the characters and the work of others? Is there no such thing as "bitterness" in the disguise of that evil sweetness with which a good man can sometimes rejoice in iniquity; hearing, perhaps, with positive satisfaction of inconsistencies of life in one from whom he has differed on questions of doctrinal truth? Be not deceived. It is one thing to be thankful that a pure jealousy for the Gospel is illustrated and vindicated, and to think prayerfully and gravely over the failures of brethren in Christ; it is another thing, and a very much easier and commoner one, to be glad because our own opinion is vindicated as such.

Is there no such thing as the very opposite of "meekness," in the form of a jealousy for our own work and reputation, which makes it disagreeable to hear of distinct blessing from God granted to work carried on in other lines than ours, or divided from ours, perhaps, by merely the demarcation that it is—not our own?

Is there no such thing as trifling, minute perhaps and subtle, but most real, with entire straightforwardness and truth; a willingness to forget that nothing can possibly be holy that is not quite truthful and quite just; that the least shadow of a "pious fraud" is great iniquity before God; that exaggerations of fact are sin, grievous sin—exaggerations, for instance, of the facts of our spiritual prosperity, or of our success in work?

And close akin to this is the sin, the contradiction to holy meekness, which lies in the least reluctance to be "brought to book" about our failures. Few things, surely, can more truly grieve the Spirit of Truth and Holiness than to see a man whom He has regenerated entrenching himself behind some personal excuse, or some theory of sanctification, against the plain duty of confessing, "I have sinned." Oh, may He never find us, and may our neighbour never find us, in such a position again; unwilling, in face perhaps of some failure of loving kindness, of charity in tone and temper, to say, "I see it; I am ashamed of myself. It need not have been, but it has been. And now, I will confess my iniquity unto the Lord, laying it on His sacred Head for pardon, and beneath His feet for victory."

Shall I touch on other things, not expressly named in this passage, but all too often known in Christian circles? Irreverence about the Name and Presence of the holy and blessed God is one of them; I have alluded to it already (p. 32). In President Edwards' account of the great revival at Northampton, in New England, early last century, there is a remarkable passage to this effect, in the complete edition of the Narrative. That revival approached, or seemed to do so, to what I know not where else to find recorded, the conversion of a whole town; and the manifestations of grace, as testified to by the great Christian thinker who wrote the story, were wonderful indeed. Describing one singularly beautiful case of fully sanctified life, he speaks of the person in question as bowed down in deep penitence under a sense of the sin involved in one mention of the name of God without adequate reverence. Such a bowing down was better than an unchastened exaltation. Take a lesson of holy Abstinence from it.*

* I hardly need say that this incident is not

Another familiar inconsistency of our Christian life, I fear, is an unthrifty use of time, that mysterious talent which, unlike other talents, does not grow, but is spent, in the using. Let us not use it with a weary anxiety, but let there be a grave habitual remembrance that it and we are in His hands for whom we exist, to whom we equally belong whether we toil or whether we rest. From useless indolence, small or great, let us totally abstain, through grace.

And let us abstain totally henceforth from the neglect of secret communion with the Lord. Nothing can take the place of that; not occasions of Christian conference, larger or more private; not

quoted to sadden or burthen one watchful, reverent believer, conscious in any true degree of the claims of the divine Majesty. Let such remember that the Holy One is "very pitiful and of tender mercy," and let them read Isai. lvii. 15, 16. Very different cases are in view here.

the intercourse of a chosen circle of pious friends; not the holy public rites and worship of the Church of God. Sooner or later, the necessity of the personal, the individual, study of the sacred Word, and of the solitary use of the Throne of grace, will assert itself, if it is slighted, in the spiritual losses of the Christian who slights it.

We have thus touched some few points which, in the experience of active and earnest Christians, if I do not mistake the case, call not seldom for a recollection of the law of the Total Abstinence of Jesus Christ. Let us recur in closing to the brief, searching, sentences of the Apostle. They penetrate in their simplicity to the centre of our being. They interdict, with the same totality of intention, not only the expression of ungoverned anger but the least swelling of internal irritation;*

* Most certainly there is such a thing in Christian life as just and wholesome indignation. The

not only the act of the adulterer, but the faintest movement of impure ideas. They prescribe an abstinence indeed. And how, oh how, in a practical sense, shall we totally abstain? There is but one reply:
Phil. iv. 13. "In Him that strengtheneth me." In Him the feeblest believer is, and He is in him, in the eternal covenant. Our need is to turn that unalterable fact into the practice of the ever-varying day and hour.

Let us look off, then, to the Lord; to
2 Cor. iii. 5. the infinity of His supply. "Our sufficiency" for an abstinence total in purpose, and in humble hope, "is of God." It is not concocted within; it is derived from above, and it is derived above all in

Christian is united to Him who not only "loveth righteousness" but "*hateth wickedness*" (Psal. xlv. 7). Only, in this as in all things let the holy Union be remembered; there will always be need to do so.

that most wonderful way, the embosoming of Jesus Christ in the very hearts of His people by the power of the Holy Comforter, through faith. With this for our secret, we may even venture to say, in sober reality, and fully alive to the realities of human life; "My Master bids me totally abstain from this or from that besetting sin. I recognize its guilt, its power. Too often have I thought it a thing for indulgence and allowance; but now I think that thought no more. And my secret for obedience, in the light of His truth, is in Himself. I lay myself, in the name of His own redemption, beneath His sacred feet. With no boastful anticipations, I yet know that for the
next step He is able to keep me from Jude 24.
stumbling, as well as hereafter to present me, as He will, faultless before the presence of His glory with exceeding joy, Amen."

III.

CHRISTIAN MODERATION.

Phil. iv. 5.—Let your moderation be known unto all men. The Lord is at hand.

THE word moderation, in this verse, is not quite self-explanatory. With "moderation" we now associate ideas, some of them excellent, some inferior, which are not the idea of the original Greek word here. Moderation means sometimes the virtue of self-government; the moderate man is the well-controlled man, whose habits and feelings in common life are his servants, not his masters. On the other hand, moderation often means what is scarcely a virtue—an abstinence, constitutional or acquired, from all extremes in opinion or practice; a "not too much," a *point de zèle*, carried into everything. The man thus moderate shuns and discountenances strong emotions, profound convictions, unsparing efforts; tends to look on evil with only a cool dislike, and on good with only a mitigated and philosophic love; is prepared to deal with great articles of faith, perhaps, as always open questions; certainly is unprepared to live and die in their defence. He dreads exceptions, and anomalies, and what is out of the main fashion of action and opinion. He prefers in everything what is called, rightly or not, "the golden mean."

Neither the virtue moderation, nor its counterfeit, is in view in this verse; most surely not the latter. Not that the Gospel here, or elsewhere, means therefore to inculcate a hot, untempered, inconsiderate enthusiasm. Indeed, enthusiasm is not a New Testament word; and no wonder, when we remember that its old connexion was with the frenzied excitements of the Greek worship of Bacchus. Enthusiasm is not indeed a word to be discarded. But yet it is a word which too often suggests hasty and ill-considered resolutions, a flow of animal excitement very likely to ebb, a heat that outruns light. And all these things are things of nature, not of grace; of fallen not of regenerate humanity. The zeal and love of the Gospel spring from deeper and purer wells, have a serener flow, and are altogether nobler things than what commonly passes under the name of enthusiasm.

But the Apostle here is looking in quite another direction. The word here rendered moderation in our Bible is connected by derivation and usage with ideas not of control, but of yielding. It is rendered *Lindigkeit*, yieldingness, giving way, in Luther's German Bible; and I fully believe the interpretation to be right. "Forbearance," "gentleness," are the alternative renderings of our Revised Version, and both suggest the thought of giving way. "Let your yieldingness be known unto all men; the Lord is near."

St Paul is dealing throughout this passage with certain holy conditions necessary to an experience of "the peace of God keeping the heart and thoughts in Christ Jesus." Standing fast in the Lord, harmony and mutual helpfulness in the Lord, rejoicing in the Lord, and prayerful and thankful communion with the Lord, are among these conditions. And with them, in the midst of them, appears this also; "Let your yieldingness be known unto all men; the Lord is near." This connexion with the deep peace of God throws a glory over the

Phil. iv. 1-7

word and the precept. The yieldingness which is here enjoined is nothing akin to weakness, indolence, or indifference. It is a positive grace of the Spirit; it flows from the fulness of Jesus Christ.

What is it? We shall find the answer partly by remembering how, from another point of view, the Gospel enjoins, and knows how to impart, the most resolute *un*yieldingness. If anything can work the great miracle of making a weak character strong, it is the Gospel. Like nothing else, it can make the victim of sensual temptation turn his back decisively upon it. It can make the weak spirit which has habitually "saved itself trouble" by falsehood—and the merest avoidance of "trouble" is the motive of numberless falsehoods—immoveably loyal to truth, at all costs to ease. It can make the regenerate will say "no" to self on a hundred points where never anything but "yes" was heard before. Nothing in the moral world is so immoveable as the will of a living Christian, sustained by the power of God the Holy Spirit, on some clear case of principle. I lately read of the uncompromising decision of a Christian man, in high military command in India, fifty years ago. He had accepted office, and £10,000 a year, being far from rich meanwhile in private means, on the condition that he should not be asked to give official countenance to idolatry. The condition was not observed. He was required to sign a grant of money to an idol temple. The East India Company would not give way, nor would their distinguished servant. He resigned his command promptly, and came home without a murmur, and without a compensation.*

Here, in a conspicuous case, was the

* *See* the *Church Missionary Intelligencer*, August, 1887.

*un*yieldingness of the Gospel, a mighty grace which, thank God, is being daily exemplified in His sight in a thousand smaller instances.

Yet this very case equally well illustrates from another side the yieldingness of the Gospel. From the point of view of principle this admirable Christian was fixed as a rock, as a mountain; from the point of view of self-interest he was moveable as air. That it was a sacrifice of self's gain and glory to resign was as nothing in his path. His interests were his Master's. Jesus Christ was in him where by nature self is. He was jealous and sensitive for the Lord; indifferent, oblivious, for himself. If I understand aright, he did not resign with a flourish of trumpets, so to speak; he did not do it sullenly or bitterly; he did not come home in that most unhappy and inglorious character—a man with a personal grievance. Quietly, and in the way of Christian business, he withdrew from a post where he could not be loyal to his King and Saviour; this was all.

Yieldingness, in our passage, is in fact SELFLESSNESS. It is meekness, not weakness; the attitude of a man out of whom the Lord has cast the evil spirit of self. It is the discovery and practice of the blessed secret how to put Jesus Christ upon the throne of life, and let that divine fact within work upon the life without. It is the grace which manifests itself in a calm, bright, willing superiority of thought and purpose to considerations of self's comfort, credit, influence. It is the noble, the blessed readiness to rejoice, for instance, in the success of others in the field of Christian work, as simply and naturally as in our own. It is the aim not to get a reputation, but to walk and please God; not to

secure the applause of others, but to compass their good and blessing; not to vindicate our opinion, but only and purely our Lord's word and truth; not to be first, but where He would put us—second, or third, or hundredth, if it is His will; not to get our rights for our sake, but to be loyal to His claims, and attentive for His sake, with scrupulous and kindly attention, to the rights and wants of others. It is a grace passive in form, if I may borrow a phrase of grammar,
1 Cor. xiii. but active in meaning. It is holy Charity, at her work of suffering long and being kind; envying not, vaunting not herself, seeking not her own, being not easily provoked, not reckoning up the evil, rejoicing with the truth, bearing, believing, hoping, enduring, all things, in the path of the will of God, the path of service of His Son.

It is a blessed thing to be a "moderate" in this sense. A living calm pervades that soul. A thousand anxieties, and a thousand regrets, incident to the life of self, are spared it. It is at leisure from itself, and therefore free for many a delightful energy and enterprise when God calls it in that direction, as well as ready for imprisonment and apparent inutility when that is His will.

An example in point rises before me. I will name no name, for that would severely pain the "moderate man" I have in view. It is a life overflowingly active of which I am thinking; a mind and will quick to originate, vigorous to execute; a heart large in sympathies and in power of influence. But never, during the observation of years, have I been able to detect in this Christian's words and works the presence of selffulness. The enterprises of others for God seem to be as interesting to him as his own. The success of his own seems to have no interest apart from that of serviceableness to Christ and His cause. And if failure ever comes it leaves no bitterness, for the effort was out of relation to self.

This is not a very common characteristic of life and work in Christian circles. Alas, how often do we see, perhaps how often we ourselves present, the opposite! Let us put it down plainly before us that this is grievous sin, direct contradiction to the Gospel in its first principles, a most certain *antidote* to the peace of God which passeth understanding, and a stumbling-block, a scandal, disastrous beyond all our reckoning, in its effects on observers.

Nothing does the world's microscope discover more keenly than selffulness in a Christian man or woman. Nothing at once baffles its experience and explanation, and attracts its notice and respect, like the genuine selflessness, the yieldingness, of the grace of God. Let ours, then, "be known unto all men"; not paraded and thrown into an attitude, but kept in practice and use in real life, where it can be put to real tests.

And would we read something, in this same verse, of its heavenly *secret?* It lies before us; "the Lord is near." He is near, not here in the sense of coming soon, but in that of standing by; in the sense of His presence, and "the secret" of it, around His servant. The very words used here by St Paul occur in this connexion in the Septuagint (Greek) translation of the Old Testament, a translation old even in St Paul's time; "Thou art near (ἐγγύς), O Lord." The thought is of the calm and overshadowing of His recollected and realized Presence; that divine atmosphere in which bitter things, and things narrow with the contractions and distortions of self, must die

Psal. xxxi. 20.

Psal. cxix. 151.

and in which all that is sweet and loving lives. "From the provoking of all men, from the strife of tongues," there is divine protection and concealment there. Let us watch and pray over our recollection of that "nearness," and we too shall learn, not by direct effort but by derivation through the Holy Spirit from Christ the Fount of Grace, to be "moderates," with a "moderation known of all men."

Psal. xxxi. 20 (Prayer Book).

St Paul himself beautifully exemplifies his own words, in this same Epistle, in the first chapter. The "brethren" at Rome who "preached Christ of envy and strife, supposing to add affliction to his bonds," certainly took a very irritating line of action. And their action tried St Paul. But it did not irritate him. He saw, condemned, and deplored their motives. But he was not angry, he was not "hurt." On the contrary,

Phil. i. 15-18.

he rejoiced. And why? Because, in however circuitous a way, the interests of Jesus Christ were being served. "Christ is being preached, and I therein do rejoice." The Lord was indeed near to His servant, near in the depths of his soul and will; and "moderation" could not but fill him in that presence.

Christian teacher, Christian worker, Christian partner, parent, student, servant, whosoever you are—"see that you abound in this grace also." Forget it, and there will be a flaw running across all your life and work for your beloved Lord. Remember it, in remembering Him, and you shall glorify Him indeed, and "sow the fruit of righteousness in peace." So say I to you, so most of all say I to myself, in the name of Jesus Christ.

2 Cor. viii. 7.

Jas iii. 18.

IV.

THE WILL OF GOD.

Eph. vi. 6.—Doing the will of God from the heart.

THIS short sentence, eight words in the English, seven only in the Greek, is a wonderfully comprehensive account of the action of the Spiritual Life. Take it word by word, and every detail in it is a great principle, meant to underlie a most happy experience and practice. "*Doing*" is its first word; doing, as against dreaming; doing, in the sense of a genuine obedience, and not merely an approval, a recognition, of what claims to be obeyed. "Doing *the will of God*" is its next word; reminding the Christian that he is indeed not his own, that he exists for Another, for his Maker and Redeemer, and that his own being will never work aright, will never fulfil its true "law," will never rest, out of the line of the will of Him who has made him, has re-made him, owns him altogether, and purposes to use him. "Doing the will of God *from the heart*," or more precisely "*from the soul*," is its last word; a word which conveys at once precept and promise; bids the man seek such a "doing" as shall be not friction and fatigue but a matter of strong, warm interest and willingness, "not a sigh, but a song"; and by thus bidding him seek, assures him that he shall find; tells him that such a doing is divinely possible in the life of grace, no day-dream but a living and practical reality for "the children of the day." 1 Thess. v. 5.

Before I go further, here let me pause, as in the presence of the King, and recollect all this for myself, and reverently press it on my reader's recollection. Not one word have I written in the previous lines that is not of the alphabet of the Gospel, or at least of its one-syllable lessons for the little children of God. But monosyllables, even in an infant's lesson, can and often do convey unfathomable and pressingly important truths; and so it is with these.

The simple statements just presented, if they express to me and to my reader not only a holy theory but in some genuine measure a holy experience, are the description of a life most blessed, most peaceful, most successful and fruitful, in the Lord's own sense of fruit and of success. Let that sentence of the Apostle, or any part of it, be to us merely theory, and we shall know little indeed of the peace and joy of God. So be it not with us, not for an hour more, if it is so now.

Approaching the words in their connexion, we find a most remarkable and suggestive connexion indeed. Whom is he addressing specially here? It is the Christian slave; the man who has found Christ, or rather has been found of Him, while being the absolute property of a human owner, under the then laws of society and the state. This man had had no voice, not the faintest, in the choice of his service, of his duties, of his burthens, of his residence, of his surroundings of any sort. His purchaser might be the best of men, or the worst; he might be Philemon, he might be Felix, or Nero. He might be a believer, or a persecutor. He might be just and generous by natural character, or capricious and unfair to the last degree. The tasks he imposed upon his slave might be well adapted to the strength and character of the worker, or extremely uncongenial, trying, and exhausting. Most assuredly the Master in heaven would take account of the unfairness or cruelty, and deal with the offender in due time. But meanwhile the slave or man, who was also the believing bondservant of the Lord Jesus, was to leave that wholly to his own and his human master's Master, and to accept the conditions of his servitude, however uneasy, as the conditions under which he was to do the will of God from the soul. Doubtless occasions for disobedience might arise; for the earthly master might possibly order him to sin. But this was a matter by itself; this would be a question not of the pleasantness or bitterness of his surroundings, the weight or lightness of his yoke, but of right and wrong, of the will and preferences not of self but of Jesus Christ. As regarded everything else that fell in his way in slavery, as regarded caprice and violence, tasks beyond his strength, uncongenial to his nature, tasks never raised perhaps above the lowest or apparently most useless level, he was to recognize in it all the will of God, and do it from the soul.

The abstract question whether slavery was right or no was never presented by the Gospel to the slave, though the precepts addressed to the master must often have suggested the question to *him*. No, the Gospel never taught revolution, though its inmost principles were pregnant with peaceful and just reform. It at once contented and ennobled the slave-convert by glorifying the actual conditions of his life with the surprising truth that, as the world stood then, they were for him the will of God, and that in accepting and fulfilling them he was serving in blessed truth the eternal Master.

It is plain from the New Testament that in countless cases this was grasped, welcomed, and lived out by human souls, through grace. Though the Apostles said not one word about emancipation, they made great multitudes of converts among slaves. We infer with wonder and joy, from the Epistles, that the life of God, the life lived by faith in the Son of God, the life of peace, and purity, and heavenly love, was lived in the slave-circle of many a household, large and small, in that corrupted classic world.

Not merely in the gaps and breathing-times of their servile duties, but in the duties and through them, multitudes of saints supernaturally saw the will of Him who had shone upon their darkness, and transfigured them into His own children.

Dwelling where an apparent iron Destiny had fixed them, they yet found in it liberty and choice, for it was to them no longer fate but the will of God. Moving up and down in their compulsory surroundings, they found themselves abiding in Jesus Christ. Taking the orders of their Greek or Latin owner, or those of his underlings, they heard through them the voice of the will of God. Were they instructions for honourable occupation, and kindly given? This was well, and welcome. Were the orders vexatious in matter, or manner, or both? Here indeed was call for the miracle of grace and power; but a call never in vain, if the heart was indeed given up to God and abiding in His Son. "His grace was sufficient for them." He shone as the First Cause through the cloud of the second. The mistakes of man were but the vehicle for the unerring touch of the love of God. Through man's unkindness, or positive malevolence, He who "loveth righteousness and hateth wicked-

2 Cor. xii. 9.

Psal. xlv. 7.

ness" was however carrying out nothing but His will through and on His saint. The soul which, by the Spirit, recollected and rested upon that truth might tabernacle in the body of the most oppressed of bondmen, but it was possessed of a peace and liberty undreamed of by the serene Stoic. For its refuge was not in itself but in Jesus Christ; in His power, not in its own; in His will, not in its own.

Such blessed lives—were they not blessed indeed then, as they are eternally blessed now in the life of glory?—St Paul contemplates, takes for granted, and writes for, in this passage. He knows that the experience is not visionary, for he knows these slaves as Christians indeed. That is to say, he knows them as redeemed, regenerated, sanctified. He knows them as Christ's purchased ones, ransomed with the blood of the Lamb, and united by the Holy Spirit to the plenitude of their

Redeemer's life and power. They were
human, mortal, sinful. Of themselves
they could do nothing. But they were
in union with Christ by grace, and by
grace they could receive out of Him "all
sufficiency" for all actual demands, for all
the will of God expressed in circumstances.
Each one of them was "joined unto the 1 Cor.
Lord, one Spirit." Therefore, "in Him vi. 17. Phil.
that strengtheneth, they could do all iv. 13.
things—all things of the will of God in Eph.
Christ Jesus concerning them." His com- ii. 10.
mandments were for them no longer 1 Joh.
"grievous," not because of their strength of v. 3.
resolution and long-practised fortitude, but
because their will was most meekly yielded
up to their beloved Possessor and Life.
Were they not blessed? Was not their
life one of far more than imperial liberty,
wealth, and peace?

I have written on, and on, about this case of the slave of old. But it has been because for myself I feel that every realized detail of that case bears with wonderful directness, *à fortiori*, upon that of each Christian in real life now. It is difficult to imagine the lot and path in which we may not feel that the argument to us from them, those dear elder brethren at Ephesus, is strong and tender indeed.

Believer in the same Lord who enabled them to do His will from the heart, can He not enable you, here and now, to do that will from your heart in your surroundings? Are you sorely tried by those surroundings? Are they in themselves humiliating to you, or exasperating to you? Are they full of acute heart-pangs, or heavy with a chronic heart-ache? Is your sphere of work and influence seemingly very narrow? Is the exterior of your daily duties very secular, very earthly? Not one of these things is for-

gotten before your Lord. Your slightest pain finds response in His sympathy. But let that thought be but the stepping-stone to this, that for you as for the slave-saint of Ephesus there lies open in that same Lord the blessed secret of a life which shall move amidst these same unwelcome surroundings as a life free, and at leisure, and at peace, full of love and rest, blessed and blessing; a life hid with Christ in God; a life in which *everything*, from your rising up to your lying down, private trial and anxiety, wrong or peril in Church or State, the smallest cross and the largest, is seen in the light of the holy, the beloved, will of God, and so is met not with a sigh, or a murmur, but "from the soul." "The will of God, done from the soul," shall be to you—yes, indeed, it shall be—a whisper of life unto life. You *have* "yielded yourself Rom. vi. 13.
to Him, as one that is alive from the

dead"; what are these things, while they last, but opportunities, dear opportunities for His sake and in His peace, of expressing that holy *fait accompli*?

Not for one moment are you asked to live thus upon the resources of nature.
Joh xv. 5. "Without Him you can do—nothing."
Phil. But it is "God who is," not only who
ii. 13. may be, "working in you, both to will, and to do, for the sake of His good pleasure," for the sake of His blessed will. Recollect that fact, and find in it a transfigured life.

"The will of God"! Let us, to animate and endear every thought of it, remind ourselves often of its blissful purposes. True, it is sovereign; let us bow low before its sovereignty, its irresponsible and unknown ways. But in all its infinite range it is the will of Him whom we know in Jesus Christ, and who has told us such gracious things about it through

Jesus Christ. If it wills for us immediately toil and trial, contradictions, disappointments, tears—as it sometimes does, as it once did for our Lord and Life—what does it always will ultimately, and with infinite skill and power to attain its end? It wills, He wills, "that not one of His little ones should perish." He wills "that every one that seeth the Son and believeth on Him should have everlasting life, and be raised up again by Christ Jesus at the last day." He wills "our sanctification." He wills, as His Son wills, that they whom He has "given" to His Son should "be with Him where He is, to behold His glory."

Matt. xviii. 14

Joh. vi. 40

1 Thess. iv. 3.

Joh. xvii. 24.

In belonging to such a God, for every part and detail of our lives, is there not both peace and glory? In accepting, loving, bearing, doing, the will of such a God is there not a blissful light upon every step of our road home? That road, even step by step, was trodden before us

by the Son of Man, who took on Him
the form of a bondservant, of a slave—
Phil. ii. 7. the Apostle boldly uses the word—the
slave of the will of His Father.

As He came down to tread it, He said,
Psal. xl. 8. "I delight to do Thy will, O my God."
Joh. iv. 34. As He trode it, He said, "My meat is to
do the will of Him that sent me, and to
Luke xxii. 42. finish His work; Not my will but Thine
be done." And it is He who by His
Spirit dwells in us, and we in Him.

Lord Jesus Christ, who thus workest in me, work on and evermore, work now, both to will and to do; to will now not my choice but Thine; to do now Thy will from the soul. Amen.

V.

PLEASURE IN INFIRMITIES.

THE subject of our last chapter connects itself with this, as the whole with the part. We have looked upon "circumstances" in their entirety as representing, as conveying, to the Christian the will of God. Here we have before us a special class of circumstances, or of conditions under which we meet them.

In 2 Cor. xii. 7, 8, 9, we read a passage full of manifold instruction about the ways of Christ with His people in their life of grace and faith. St Paul has been spiritually privileged to a degree inconceivable without the same experience. He has been present, it matters not how, in the

Third Heaven, in Paradise, and has heard words there not to be reported by a mere human being; words, very possibly, expressive of eternal kindness and approval towards himself and his work. He returns from this more than Tabor to the plain of common life. And he is put at once under severe discipline; "the thorn in the flesh," "the buffeting angel of Satan," is "given to him." Yes, this
Phil. i. 29. was the next "gift on behalf of Christ." And, as if to make thorn and buffeting more unbearable, we might think, it was intimated somehow to him that this was all done, all assigned by his Master, for a reason most humiliating. It was "lest he should be exalted above measure"; it was to check personal vanity in advance, to prevent something coming up in his experience which otherwise would have come up—self-satisfaction. Such was St Paul, it thus appeared, that strong mea-

sures on Jesus Christ's part were needed, in an acmé of spiritual experience, if he was not thus to sin.

Such a fact, painfully real for the Apostle then, speaks an abiding word of holy humiliation to all true believers, since and now. It is manifestly written "for our learning," and says to us that Rom.xv. 4.
"this infection of nature doth remain, yea in them that are regenerated."* True, it has been argued—I have heard it so argued—that even St Paul's experience is not to be our standard; that we should aim, in Christ, to rise above even it! And there is thus much truth in this, that most surely the only true standard of inner principle and outer practice is the Lord. But then, when the Holy Spirit instructs an Apostle to record his own experience *as part of a passage of instruction*, as here, it is obvious that the experi-

* Art IX. of the Church of England.

ence is meant to embody and illustrate permanent truth. The Lord is, as ever, the unaltered standard. He, who needed no discipline to keep HIM meek and lowly, is the standard; and we are in Him. Nevertheless, we gather hence that it is a permanent fact of the life of grace and faith on earth that, notwithstanding our being in Him, we need His discipline to keep us low. It is meant to keep us low; it can do so; accepted, it will do so. But let His hand be taken off, and self will re-
Gal. v. 17. appear indeed. It "lusteth," it tendeth,
"against the Spirit" still.

Let us not be discouraged. Our souls are touched from above—and from within, for it is by the Indweller—with that desire, longing, and choice for conformity to Him which nothing but Himself can satisfy. But let us not be discouraged by the Holy Spirit's intimation here that "this infection of nature doth remain."

In the very recognition of this humiliating fact on the witness of the Holy Word, in a meek submission to this condition, mystery that it is, there can come to the soul a direct gift of sanctifying peace and power.

Even thus, as this passage clearly indicates, St Paul found it to be. He thrice asked the Lord, the Master, to remove the thorn, to forbid the buffets. And He who knew St Paul better than he knew himself, though he had been in heaven, said no. It was to remain. I think we gather that it was lastingly, at least indefinitely, to remain. Whatever was the pang, the burthen, the restraint, the hindrance (and doubtless he said much to the Lord about this, for see Phil. iv. 6), he was to go on with it, and to know all the time why he was to do so; lest he should be exalted above measure.

But now comes in the glorious other

side of the matter. The prayer was never granted. But how fruitful was that prayer! It was denied, yet answered. The Master's "no" was not a mere peremptory negative, decisive and perfectly authoritative as it was. It took the form of a positive assurance inestimably better; the form not only of a promise, let us observe, but of a present certainty of divine life and love. "My grace is sufficient for thee; for my strength is made perfect in weakness." The weakness, of whatever special kind, so profoundly, so intensely felt by St Paul, so destructive in itself of his comfort, so obstructive in his work, was to be no unfavourable condition from his Master's point of view. It was rather the true condition under which the Master's indwelling strength was to work out its proper issues, so that "the patient" gave himself up to the process. And so, what was "sufficient" for St Paul's peace, and strength, and growth, was—not the removal of the humiliating thorn *and* the grace of Christ, but simply, merely, the grace of Christ, that is to say Christ, by His Spirit, divinely present and divinely working in St Paul. Yes, this was enough for the whole demands of the case. It was sufficient up to the level of the need. It was adequate to take the whole circumstances, and fill them all with peace, with power, with love, with God.

"My grace IS sufficient for thee." I have heard of a life in which that sentence was a great spiritual turning point. In the midst of an agonizing prayer, "Let Thy grace be sufficient for me," the eyes of the overwhelmed Christian were casually raised towards a text upon the wall, where this sentence appeared. The word "IS" stood out conspicuous in colour. And with the sight of it came, through the Spirit, the simple but divine intuition that what was implored was possessed already. Reader, have you read that "IS"? Does your experience this hour include faith that rests as well as seeks? If so, is it not a sacred, a blessed reality? If not so, why not? Here is the warrant, phrased in the present tense, and the words are your MASTER's, your Possessor's, words. Believe them now—that is to say, practically, act upon them now.

St Paul did so. It is a delightful "therefore" with which he pursues his story. "Most gladly *therefore*," therefore, because the Lord has said this, just for that reason, "will I glory in my infirmities, that the power of Christ may rest upon me, may (literally) tabernacle upon me," as the Shechinah-cloud upon the camp of Israel. And further, "*Therefore* I take pleasure in infirmities, in reproaches, in necessities, in persecutions, for Christ's sake; for when I am weak, then am I strong."

How far does he stand beyond mere resignation, in its ordinary sense! He does not merely endure; he does not merely go on with a sigh, which would signify a longing for other circumstances.
Ah, he knows what sighs, what groans Rom. viii. 23
are. But for him, surely, they have be- 2 Cor. v. 4.
come things not of the *inmost* depth; not of the spiritual centre. The central consciousness now, in Christ, who is in him, is a profound and holy pleasure in the Lord's choice of circumstances, because they are chosen to serve the Lord's purposes, and to develope His power. "I take pleasure in infirmities."

Christian reader, is it so with you? Let me not assume that it is not. Thanks be to God, in all ages of His Church it has been so with many souls, who have learnt by grace the divine secret, the open secret, of the peace of simplicity, simplicity of relations with God in Christ as at once Father and Possessor. And in our own day a growing number of His people are entering with more and more distinctness into what is meant by this holy simplicity; not craving some new truth, but applying new trust to the old.

So I will assume that I speak to one who knows something of this chastened and Christian "pleasure." Is it not a holy, a healthy thing, a thing of the daylight? Is it not wonderful in its elasticity, its solidity, its repose, its freedom? You have read of saints who, well qualified for active life and extended influence, have been shut up for long and rigorous imprisonments in days of persecution, such days as may return to us, and are abundantly possible now in many a distant land. To them, as you have read, strange and sweet joys have sprung out of their terrible restriction. Seeing in man's wrong and cruelty the mere implement in their Lord and Father's hand, they have mysteriously but really rejoiced in the cell, in the dungeon. "The stones of my prison walls," says one saint, Madame de la Mothe Guyon,* "have often seemed as rubies in my eyes." And this was no illusion of an excited brain, but the calm inference of a life hidden with Christ, and profoundly content to be a subject of His will and grace.

Well, the joy and peace of the martyr and confessor is a thing translatable, as you know, into the experience of very common days. What are *your* prison walls? Broken health, failing limbs,

* Madame Guyon undoubtedly was not exempt from errors, Romanist and other. But her sorrows and sufferings were due, above all things, to her testimony to the need and possibility of living a life hid with Christ in God.

while you would choose to be all movement for God? Aching head, weary nerves, while it is your duty to be surrounded with toil and bustle? A sphere of service curiously unlike what you would have chosen, in view of your knowledge of your own capacities or weakness, yet in which you are to-day, and out of which your Lord does not—at least to-day—lead you? Home service, where you would prefer to be a missionary pioneer? A parish, when you would like to evangelize a province? A sick-room to fill with patient service, when you would like to organize a hospital? Study, when you would like out-door preaching? Out-door preaching, when you would choose study? A life of entirely secular conditions, when you would choose the holy ministry? Limited abilities, difficulty of speech, when you would like to be able, eloquent, for Christ? Poverty, when your heart aches for riches that you may spend for Him? Riches, when you would fain have done, for His sake, with their solemn responsibilities, and be free in the restful simplicity of humbler life? Surroundings marred by the mistakes and perhaps injustice of others, while you long for co-operation and intelligent, healthy sympathy?

You know, in all these things, what it is to "take pleasure." They are delightful, not in themselves, but from this poin of view. The restraint, the negative, has become blessed to you, for it is your Lord's chosen opportunity for saying to you, "My grace is sufficient for thee." Your former fret and "worry" under circumstances are gone; for circumstances are literally as full as they can hold of occasions for the acceptance and working of His power. You would rather be weak, and the subject of His power, than be strong. You would rather be at uncongenial work, and have it filled with Him, than be at your most darling occupation, of your own mere will. In the mistakes, in the wrongdoings of man you yet see and welcome the unmistaking love and wisdom of your Lord. Your deep, calm, silent desire is that He should be glorified in you. And as this is manifestly, very often, best done "in your infirmities," you can, you do, in Him, take pleasure in them. For infirmities of every scale, for little as for great, for great as for little, by a blessed inclusion, His grace is sufficient.

It is no exhausting process; so severe an effort to-day that it can scarcely be expected to be sustained to-morrow. It is not the emission so much as the reception of spiritual power. It is a profound contact with your Head, your life; "Jesus, your strength, your hope."

It does not make you a visionary, or a fanatic. If trying circumstances change in some respects, you reasonably welcome the change, and remember that pain is never for *its own sake* good. But you have reaped, and reap, such disclosures of the Lord's power out of "infirmities," out of "distresses," great or little, that you cannot help a certain love for them, for the sake of what goes with them. And so, if it is "given to you on behalf of Christ" to suffer special trial, of body, Phil. i. 29.
mind, means, work, surroundings of whatever sort, you meet it with a quiet welcome, and expect His overshadowing.

> "'Tis your happiness below
> Not to live without the Cross;
> But your Saviour's power to know,
> Sanctifying every loss."

VI.

CONFLICT AND PEACE.

Eph. vi. 10–18.—Finally, my brethren, be strong in the Lord, and in the power of His might. Put on the whole armour of God, that ye may be able to stand against the wiles of the devil. For we wrestle not against flesh and blood, but against principalities, against powers, against the rulers of the darkness of this world, against spiritual wickedness in high places. Wherefore take unto you the whole armour of God, that ye may be able to withstand in the evil day, and having done all, to stand. Stand therefore, having your loins girt about with truth, and having on the breastplate of righteousness; and your feet shod with the preparation of the gospel of peace; above all, taking the shield of faith, wherewith ye shall be able to quench all the fiery darts of the wicked. And take the helmet of salvation, and the sword of the Spirit, which is the word of God: praying always with all prayer and supplication in the Spirit, and watching thereunto with all perseverance and supplication for all saints.

Phil. iv. 7.—And the peace of God, which passeth all understanding, shall keep your hearts and minds through Christ Jesus.

THE title of this chapter presents a contrast, but it is a contrast full of harmony. The Peace and the Conflict of the believing Christian are things intended, in their true idea, not to take each other by turns, but to be intertwined, to bear habitually upon one another, to make the secret of one tenor of life, and that a life of chastened happiness. Let us look into the matter, in a brief study of the conflict and of the peace in question.

I.

THE CHRISTIAN'S CONFLICT.

Consider this first, and in the light of the passage quoted at the head of the chapter; with the recollection that it is a subject not only of importance, but of vital im-

Deut. xxxii. 47. portance, to every disciple. It is indeed "our life."

1. The Ephesian passage asks to be read with full remembrance, first, of its CONNEXION. Have you ever remarked that connexion? To many readers, I believe, this picture of armour and soldier calls up the thought of dark and terrible external strife. It suggests, perhaps, the resolute confessor of Christ bracing himself to meet Satan in his open wrath; on some day of persecution, with its tribunal, its prison, its scaffold, or its fire; or at least at some time of peculiarly vehement and angry temptation of other sorts; amidst which the saint is solitary and terrified, and almost forcibly overborne. But as a fact the passage comes in, naturally and in sequence, to close and crown a long series of directions how to live at home, how to please the redeeming Lord in the sphere of home duties. Husband, wife, child,

parent, master, servant—these are the words which have led up to the thought of the armour, the conflict, and the dark foes who press round the believer in the field.

Is this unnatural? It is indeed surprising for the moment, but not unnatural. I appeal to the heart of my reader, taking it for granted that for most of my readers the lot is cast, wholly or partly, in the life of an English home, or in some life closely akin to it; and I ask, is not home too often the scene of our greatest spiritual failures, our most manifest inconsistencies, our least resistance to the enemy, and accordingly his greatest successes over us? It is a deep fact, a far-reaching fact, that just where the path looks most commonplace and easy the enemy of our spiritual life is likely to set his most subtle ambush. Where we are habitually least upon our guard he is habitually most upon the watch. And then, on the other hand, this scene of so much possible failure is therefore capable, through grace, of being the scene of delightfully frequent and fruitful victory, victory of that gentle, humble and unobtrusive kind which is the truest and the strongest after all.

2. Thus much about the connexion. Think next of the ENEMIES presented to our thought by St. Paul. What are they, who are they? In our Baptism we were dedicated and sealed to a manful warfare against an unholy triple Alliance—"the world, the flesh, and the devil;" and we shall have to deal with all the three even to the end. But the present passage isolates, as it were, the third member of the alliance, and deals with it alone. It presents us with the fact of personal spirits of evil, under their great head and chief, actively at work and at war against us. In one respect, such a view includes

within it the remembrance of the world and the flesh. For the personal evil powers, assuredly, to a degree greater than we ever realize, organize and energize the attack, from whatever quarter it comes. Diabolus, in the pages of that wonderful book, Bunyan's *Holy War*, knew how to attack from without, both by assault, and by parley with weak or treacherous inmates of the Town of Mansoul. But not to pursue this thought, we have as a fact a host of unseen personal spirits put here before us as our foes. They are indeed real persons, not figures of speech, say the contrary who will. True, they are an awful mystery, but a mystery not greater *in kind* than is the existence of evil *men* who live, as many do, to tempt others into evil. In anywise, to the Lord and to His Apostles they were "a living, *dark* reality." In the Word of God the Christian's conflict is seen to be one not merely "with flesh and blood," that is to say with frail mortal men, withstanding and tempting, but against this dark throng of unseen assailants, working personally, and working earnestly, in quiet as well as in alarming hours, for his spiritual loss and woe.

3. Observe next the precise and definite AIM of these adversaries. It is to dislodge you, Christian, from a point on which you stand, on which you are set and stationed by your Lord. You see yourself here as a soldier, but not as a soldier on the march through a hostile country, nor as running the errands of your Captain, but as posted upon a vantage-ground in the field. The strategy of the enemy aims above all things at getting you to leave it. We all know how the day of Hastings was lost, and the history of England changed for ever, by a failure—not to manœuvre, to march, to charge,

but to stand, having done all to stand, within a vantage-ground. Every day brings for the soul its field of Hastings. Forewarned, let us secure victory. Let us stand, withstand, having done all let us stand.

4. Remember next what the POINT OF VANTAGE is, from which we are to pray and watch that He who keeps us "will Psal.
not suffer our feet to be moved." The cxxi. 3.
tenth verse of our chapter informs us; all-important information! It is nothing less than "THE LORD." "Stand fast in (not only near, but in) the Lord, and in the power of His might." Weigh the words well. Let them not pass as a mere sacred phrase, a mere formula of the religious dialect. They are concerned with the central facts of our spiritual life and power. "In the Lord" lies your secret, our secret, of love, and peace, and joy; of victory and progress; of heavenly

temper in earthly duty; of all we need for life and work in His name. Union with our glorious Redeemer and Head, wrought in us by that Holy Spirit through whom we were born again; communion with Christ Jesus, wrought in us by that same Spirit as He leads us on; all this lies hidden "in the Lord."

The phrase, in the present connexion, speaks specially of the life of communion with Him, union realized and put into use; communion not only at His sacred and happy Table, but in all ways and at all times of definite spiritual contact with Jesus Christ. This contact, this "keeping in
Joh. xv. 4. touch," this abiding in Him is, practically, our strength and vantage-ground; and to draw us from it, into the plain, into the vale of Siddim full of slime pits, is the strength and advantage of the enemy. Let him drive us or entice us thence, let him meet us out of contact with our Lord, and he

will have the victory, whether it be on a day of persecuting terror or on a day of amplest home comfort and charming surroundings. Let us stand then, and be strong, in the Lord. Let us keep our communion with Jesus Christ clear and full. Let us, not now and then, but in a blessed growth of habit, carry all our needs to Him and draw all our power from Him. Let us remember the power of the little word "now," and do this NOW. Nothing is too great for our Maker's strength; nothing is too small for His attention.

Keep the vantage-ground, and "put on"—what lies always ready upon it—"the whole armour of God." Every piece of that panoply means, in effect, Jesus Christ believed in and brought to bear upon the foe. Observe this not least in the case of the soldier's *shoes*; "the preparation," that is, the *equipment*, "of the Gospel of peace"; the arming of the Christian's feet with that strong appropriation of "peace with God through our Lord Jesus Christ," which gives foothold indeed as we stand upon the Rock. But against every variety of need array yourself with Jesus Christ. He is both fort and armour. And He has overcome, and we in Him. The enemy who surges around us is real, is fierce; but he is only fighting on after defeat; a beaten, a broken, army. Let us stand where we are already set, and use what we wear, and be calmly confident of success, with glory for its end.

II.

THE CHRISTIAN'S PEACE.

As we turn to this delightful branch of the subject, let us read again the language of Phil. iv. 7: "The peace of God, which passeth all understanding, shall keep (lit., shall garrison) your hearts and minds, in

Christ Jesus." The harmony in contrast, of which I spoke in the first words of the chapter, is suggested, is explained, by that quotation. We have just been contemplating a battle-field, and its critical point, held by the Christian, assailed by his spiritual foes. We look at it, so to speak, from the outside, and it is a fort, an entrenchment, surrounded by a tide of battle. Here we are given a view of the interior, and we see its defender, its maintainer, amidst that angry tide, nevertheless in peace, kept in peace, garrisoned and sentinelled with peace. Occupying a position in its nature impregnable, and using weapons in their nature impenetrable and infallible, he stands, he resists, he engages the foe with the sword, yet in the strong tranquillity of the possession of advantage and the certainty of victory. Like Elisha in Dothan, he sees the Syrians, 2 Kings
and knows that they are no vision of a vi. 17.

dream, but formidable invaders, bent upon his mischief. But he sees also, with the eye of faith, a living circle of fortification and garrison between him and them; chariots and horses of fire; the peace of God, the God of peace.

To lay aside the military imagery, suggested probably in both places to St Paul by the Roman soldiery with whom he was so long familiar—he was actually chained to a Pretorian when he wrote these words—the Philippian passage reminds us that the believer's triumph in daily life over temptation, over the power of the enemy, is intended, in the plan of God, to be an experience full of peace. Fluctuations in success there may be. Nay, in the mysterious fact of our imperfection here, our imperfection of reception, there not only may but must be a falling "short of the glory of God," occa-

Rom. iii. 23. sions very many for profound and tender

confession of sin. But this is no part of the plan of God. From the point of view of His provision, there is planned for us and offered to us nothing less than a continuous deliverance, a calm unbroken standing on the hill of victory, a long experience of peace passing understanding, keeping the heart and mind in Christ Jesus. "Change" in *these* things is not "our *portion* here," in the sense of an allotment from above. What the eternal Shepherd prepares, apportions, and allots, is "a table, in the presence of our enemies." Psal. xxiii. 5.

One of the most tranquil and happy deaths of which I have ever heard was that of a young English officer in one of the battles of the Soudan. He was struck by an Arab shot, and expired in the midst of the square, walled in by his men, while the savage assailants beat upon their ranks in vain; yielding up his soul there in the deliberate calm of faith to the Lord of Life. Some parable we may see in this of what may be the quiet intercourse with Jesus Christ enjoyed by the inmost heart of the Christian while temptation flies thickest around him, so that he meets it in and with the Lord. This chapter of the Epistle to the Philippians is full of suggestions in that direction. "In the Lord" is its key-note also, as well as that of the message to the Ephesians. "Stand fast in the Lord"; "be of the same mind in the Lord"; "rejoice in the Lord"; "the peace of God shall keep you, in Christ Jesus."

Observe, as we pass on, the phraseology of the verse. It is that of promise. Sweet is the sound of "the peace of God" when uttered at the close of Sabbath worship; when spoken after the heavenly Communion Feast. But there it is a benediction, a holy invocation; here it is more, it is a promise; not "may it," but "it shall." Such a thing then as this peace of God there is, and is meant to be, in the experience not of some but of all watchful believers, of all who "stand in the Lord," their strength. It is guaranteed to them. They are invited humbly to claim it, and to possess it, under the Covenant of peace.

Yes, remember this, busy and burthened disciple; man or woman tried by uncertain health; immersed in secular duties; forced to a life of almost ceaseless publicity, social, ministerial, or however it may be. Here is written an assurance, a guarantee, that not at holy times and welcome intervals only, not only in the dust of death, but in the dust of life, there is prepared for you the peace of God, able to keep your hearts and thoughts in Christ Jesus.

It is no dead calm, no apathy. It is the peace of God; and God is life, and light, and love. It is found in Him, it is cultivated by intercourse with Him. It is "the secret of His presence." Amidst the circumstances of your life, which are the expression, as we have recollected above, of His will, He can maintain it, He can keep you in it. Nay, it is not passive; it "shall keep" you, alive, and loving, and practical, and ready at His call.

Psal. xxxi. 20.

It can, it shall, keep "the heart"—that word of such wide and inclusive significance in Scripture; the inner world of will, and affection, and understanding. It can keep "the thoughts," sweetly controlling, tempering, attuning, the actual outcome of the heart in articulate purposes and opinions. Yes, it can work miracles in these things.

In closing, I recur to our Ephesian chapter, and to that one detail in it touched on already, "the preparation, the equipment, of the Gospel of peace." I have pointed out that this puts before us the believing combatant in his strong, firm, calm appropriation of peace with God, and, let me now add, of what goes with and springs from peace *with* God—the peace *of* God, keeping the heart. Thus in the very centre of the imagery of conflict is imbedded the imagery of peace; not only a clinging to the eternal Rock, but rather an untroubled foothold upon it.

Rom v 1.

Here is peace indeed. "In the world ye shall have tribulation," but, coincidently, "in Me ye shall have peace." A Buddhist in China, converted to the Faith not many years ago, confessed his new-found Lord by saying to his friends, whenever he could, "Jesus Christ is peace to-day." Even so for us now, in our circumstances of to-day, Jesus Christ is peace. In the conditions of our actual

Joh xvi. 33.

path, in the things which lie like snares hidden in the grass of a quiet daytime, amidst our petty but perilous temptations to selfishness, to temper, to evil speaking, to vanity, to frivolity, to impure thoughts, to unfaithfulness or untruth in act and word, Jesus Christ and our communion with Him is peace. The things around are the conditions, the materials, of real assaults, and therefore of real conflicts. But they may be met from within by "Him who dwells within," with the victory of a real, a sacred, an unruffled peace. "We wrestle; therefore stand fast in the Lord."

Be on the watch, for it is war-time. Be above all things on the watch, then, over your peace in Christ. Stand in Him; arm with Him. Against all circumstances, clothe yourself in Him. All this requires, as we have seen,* the blessed diligence of secret prayer, of loving and adoring con-

* Chap. I.

verse with the Word of God, of faithful use of all the means of grace. But it means the using of them in the right direction, for the right end, so as to keep us "in touch" at all times with that living Lord who is both the victory and the peace of His people.

Then shall we have peace, and shall manifest it, and diffuse it in the very hour of conflict. "He shall not suffer our foot to be moved; He that keepeth us shall not slumber." Psal. cxxi. 3.

VII.

MANIFOLDNESS.

1 Pet. i. 6.—Manifold temptations.
1 Pet. iv. 10.—Manifold grace.
Eph. iii. 10.—Manifold wisdom.

There is an obvious contrast of subject-matter between the first of these quotations and the others. But the idea of manifoldness, variety, appears in all, and this connects them, and suggests important facts regarding the relation between the Christian's needs, and his Lord's supplies, and his Lord's purposes towards him.

i. Manifold temptations. On the word "temptation" I do not dwell at length, only remarking that the original word lends itself equally to denote the solicitations of the great Enemy and the tests of the Eternal Friend; "temptation" and "trial" respectively, in our present parlance. And it is obvious that these things are very often, perhaps always, in the case of the believer, two aspects of one thing. In the history of Job we see Satan tempting, with resolute and merciless purposes of evil; we see the Lord trying, so as to shew to his "perfect," his thoroughly genuine, servant more of the plague of his own heart, and very much more of the glory and love of God. And we see the two processes carried on in great measure by the same events and experience.

Job i. 8.

This double process is one of the normal facts of the Christian's life. The Enemy is unwearied in temptation, the Friend mercifully perseveres with the touchstone and the probe. And truly to the regenerate soul both processes have to do with pain, with heaviness. Temptation, whatever be the victory of grace over it, has this deep pain in it, that it means the presence of the foe of the soul and of its Lord. Trial, whatever be the secret joy of knowing who sends it, and why, and of learning more of Him through it, a joy on which we dwelt above,* is in its very nature painful. It is intended to hurt, though not to injure. The Lord does not make His people Stoics, but Christians. His blessing does not blunt but refine their sensibilities, while it gives strength to their weakness. They feel the rod, they feel the Refiner's fire. Not only in view of temptation, but under sense of trial, they understand what heaviness means.

Meanwhile let us remember, though but in passing, that heaviness was not the leading experience of St Peter's converts.

* Ch. V.

Their characteristic was joy and love. Read over the golden verses which contain this word about "heaviness." They form a picture radiant with the light of the Lord; with living hope, ardent love, joy unspeakable and full of glory. And St Peter speaks of these experiences as the present and habitual portion of these beloved "strangers scattered." *

On the other hand, and this is our chief concern now, this picture of light is crossed by a deep, tender shadow; "heaviness

* I well remember a friend's telling me that he had lighted upon two very different comments on this passage, almost at once. In the one, an expositor maintained that such glowing words must refer to the life to come; that they could only be anticipations of heaven, not experiences on earth. The other comment was an entry in the diary of the late Rev. W. H. Hewitson, a saint who had deep experiences of the Cross: "I have been rejoicing all day long with joy unspeakable, and full of glory.'

through manifold temptations." It is not easy, perhaps, to dissect the subject and to explain the theory. *Solvitur ambulando;* it is explained to the believing soul by a walk with God.

> "Wouldst thou too understand? Behold I show
> The perfect way: *Love God, and thou shalt know.*" *

And this experience of "heaviness" is "manifold." It has to do with manifold temptations, varied trials. Yes, they are varied, indeed. It was so of old. We have but to name the saints of Hebrews xi. to see this in its vivid reality. But it is a fact too close to the human heart of all time to need much illustration. No two of us are fully alike in character or in surroundings. No one of us is free from innumerable changes in the incidence of his surroundings on his character. Age

* James Montgomery, *The Lot of the Righteous.*

of life, social position, mental and moral education, bodily ease or disease, relationships and connexions, private and public duties,—I designedly mention these things without order, — all these differences, and how many others touching upon the individual spirit within, make up a vast "manifoldness" of temptation, of trial. And we can go only a very little way in helping one another in the multiplicity. We are like enough to another to understand the fact; we are unlike enough to be soon baffled in the details, even when we bring our best sympathy to bear. Only a little can the Christian whose trial is the snare and care of wealth enter into the life whose trial is poverty and straits; and the converse is true also. Only imperfectly can the Christian burthened with public responsibility enter into the difficulties that are bounded by the humble home. Not fully, with rare exceptions, can the strong, in health or in will, appreciate the essence of the temptations of the weak. And, again, such are the intricacies of life and of the soul, that the same man may often find himself tried at once from different quarters, on opposite sides of character. It is a manifold problem.

ii. The manifold GRACE OF GOD. Here the problem finds a blessed answer. We have studied an extremely complicated lock, and no key in all our store will meet it and move it. But the great Artificer of both circumstances and salvation appears here with His perfect key, His golden key, cast into the very mould of the labyrinthine wards, intended and able to fit them all. Need aboundeth, in
Rom v. 20. its many ramifications. But "grace doth much more abound"; it is the manifold grace of God.

True, beneath its multiplicity grace has

a divine simplicity and singleness. For what is GRACE, when we come to its ultimate description? It is no abstract thing; no mysterious substance, thrown off as it were by God and injected into man. It is the Lord Himself in action. Grace of acceptance—what is it but God, for Christ's sake, pardoning and welcoming the sinner—"GOD FOR Rom.
us"? Grace of sanctification, of peace viii. 31.
and power and holiness, what is it but
"GOD working IN us to will and to do"; Phil. ii.
"the Spirit strengthening us in the inner 13. Eph. iii.
man"; "Christ dwelling in the heart by 16, 17.
faith"? What is human kindness but a kind man in action? What is divine grace but the Lord Himself, infinitely kind, acting for, and acting in, the soul?

Thus there is a glorious oneness in the inmost idea of grace. But it is a oneness out of which springs its infinite manifoldness of fitness and application. Personal action, in its very nature, is thus manifold; and grace is divinely personal action. The most refined machine is limited to a rigid narrowness in line and scope of work; it stands utterly devoid of the power to feel and meet new circumstances. The humblest Person is capable, as such, of a boundless versatility, an endless adaptability, compared with the impersonal machine. Grace is manifold, beyond the variations of our utmost need, just because it is the action within the soul and will of Him, not it but Him, who dwells within.

Thus it meets the case, be the case what it may. Never for a moment interfering with our personality, or suspending the work and office of our conscience, it, that is to say the Lord thus present, comes self-adjusted to the trial, to the temptation, of this hour, of this minute. No craft of the enemy is too subtle for that skill. No force of circumstances is too pressing for that power. There is "no temptation with" which He cannot "make a way to escape"—into Himself. There is no labyrinth of so-called conflicting duties out of which He cannot guide into a straight path. 1 Cor x. 13.

There is abundant skill and power in grace to bring the anxious and the weak to the feet of Jesus Christ, be their antecedent obstacles what they may. There is resource in grace alike for the life of ceaseless energy and intercourse, that it may be lived in God, and for the life of solitude and forced inaction that it may be made occasion for new sacrifices to Him. There is fit provision for the temptations of the young, buoyant spirit, and for the needs of the melancholy and fearing. It, that is to say He, can so meet the case, that "the weak shall say, I am strong." It, that is to say He, "gives what He enjoins."* Joel iii. 10.

* *Da quod jubes, et jube quod vis.* St Augustine.

It, that is to say He, is adjusted to every need of life. And when the need of death comes, when the "next thing" to do is to step into the valley, to touch the edge of the cold river, grace will be found (ah, let us be sure of it, as life moves on, and the thought of death only gains in mystery as we approach it), grace will be found perfectly adjusted to that hour. And our best preparation for that need will be to welcome this holy manifoldness for the needs of this present, for this waking moment of active or suffering life. We yet shall find, through Him that loved us and abideth in us, that it is " very simple thing to die."

So let us thankfully face the multiplicityof circumstances, and of trials. Let us recognize in "the changing scenes of life" fresh occasions for the great Artificer to employ His will, His power. Let us remember that for every one of them there is, somewhere in Him who is with us and in us, the corresponding gift. The subject is endless indeed in its development. Its treatment is coextensive with our life.

iii. Now we turn from St Peter to St Paul, and hear him speak of what is manifold also; "the manifold WISDOM OF GOD."

The words have a special reference, as will be seen, of special and beautiful significance. The Apostle speaks of this manifold wisdom, not in the abstract, but as illustrated and in action in the true Church, that is to say in "the blessed company of all faithful people"; * and in the view of very important spectators. "The principalities and powers," the spirits of the heavenly world, "angels and archangels and the company of heaven," * are seen in this wonderful verse studying the

* The Communion Service.

wisdom of God as shown in the believing company. To take the simplest aspects of this disclosure of God's word ; we have it indicated here that Christians, of every grade, and character, and situation, and age, and name, are capable of thus being viewed from above, to the glory of the wisdom of their God. The poorest, humblest, most forgotten and neglected saint of Christ in whose manifold trials manifold grace is doing its work, may at this moment be affording to our "elder brethren of the sky" discoveries of what the Lord is and what He can do, most precious to themselves. In us they see what they cannot see in their own bright ranks; the victory of grace over the infinitely complicated problem of the recovery, the acceptance, the sanctification, the glory, of beings fallen, rebellious, justly condemned, and under all the conditions of the flesh.

Very different are the specimens they

study; the Christian martyr, the Christian leader and master of men, the Christian thinker and student, the missionary and evangelist, the Christian mother, the friend of the needy and the outcast, the little believing child, the lonely aged one, the dying one, sinking into what to us looks like "utter destruction,"* but what by them is seen as the triumphant issue of divine wisdom, turning death into the gate of life.

Are we part of the subject-matter of God's lessons to these heavenly learners in the study of His manifold wisdom? Is there anything in our lives from which an angel might learn more of God? If there is an ambition lawful in the life of penitent sinners, can there be a purer aspiration than that we may be used as illustrations to the minds of the Blessed, not of what man can be but of what He whom we love can do?

* See the noble passage, Wisdom iii. 1–4.

VIII.

GRACE FOR GRACE.

Joh. i. 16.—Of His fulness have all we received, and grace for grace.

Psal. xxxvi. 11.—For with Thee is the fountain of life.

In the last chapter we have had much to say about the applications of sanctifying grace, and in the last but one something of its nature. Here is a Scripture which speaks of it again, and describes a delightful special aspect of our derivation of grace from its fountain.

On the first clause of the quotation from St John I say but little. Only observe that it points to Jesus Christ as the embodi-

ment, the reservoir, the fountain, of all
that grace means for us. And it speaks ver. 12.
of the vital connexion of us, of His believing followers, with Him as a definite and
accomplished fact. "We have received,"
or, somewhat more literally, "we did
receive." Of himself and of all believers
St John says this. They have come into
receptive contact with Jesus Christ, with
the divine fulness that is in Him. "The 2 Cor. iv. 13.
Spirit of faith" has come. The work of
submissive trust has been wrought in the
soul, the trust which looks not at itself
but at the trusted One alone. Then the
soul is not only in the hands of its blessed
Rescuer; it has come into spiritual con-
tinuity with His exalted Life. "Virtue is Mar. v. 30.
gone out of Him"; His strength into
their imptconce, His peace into their
nature's war. Because He lives, they live Joh. xiv. 19.
also.

The last clause of the quotation speaks

of a certain mode, or phase, of our re-
1 Pet. iii. 7. ception of this fulness, this "grace of life" which once could not flow into us, but to which now our will, our being, thanks be to God, has opened wide the door. Let us examine it.

"Grace for grace." On the word "grace" I have said a little already,* and will not repeat it. I assume the reader's remembrance of the truth that sanctifying grace is no mere impersonal "substance," but "God working in us"; the Lord in action in our very springs of thought and will. Now observe the phrase before us here; "grace *for* grace." Quite literally —I know not how to render more exactly —the words run, "Grace *instead* of grace."

What does this mean? Surely the thought, the image, is of a perpetual succession of supply; a displacement and replacement ever going on; ceaseless

* Ch. VII.

arrivals of all that is needed for the ceaseless changes of need and demand. The picture before us is as of a river. Stand on its banks, and contemplate the flow of waters. A minute passes, and another. Is it the same stream still? Yes, assuredly, the same Thames, or Wye, that ran ages ago in our forefathers' sight. But is it the same water? No. The liquid mass that passed you a few seconds ago fills now another section of the channel; new water has displaced it, or if you please replaced it; water instead of water. And so hour by hour, and year by year, and century by century, the process holds; one stream, other waters, living not stagnant, because always in the great identity there is perpetual exchange.

Even so in the Christian's life, and in that derived fulness which is its secret of plenty and of peace. Hour comes instead of hour, joy instead of joy, snare instead of snare, trial and pain and loss instead of other like things of yesterday. But so also with the supply, the successions and exchanges of strength and blessing that come of the unchanging and unsuccessional presence in the believing man of Him whom he has received. Grace takes the place of grace; ever new, ever old, ever the same, ever fresh and young, for hour by hour, for year by year, through life.

Our verse delightfully negatives the thought of grace as a something to be stored up in our own hands on occasions; a limited supply, to be economized and managed, and made to last, till it runs dry, or almost dry, and must be replenished by some new means. Here it flows for us, by us, in us, for evermore; ever
Lam. iii 22. passing, ever abiding, "new every morning, failing not," for the soul which is in contact with the eternal source.

Let us go forth in peace, in the peace

which is itself a power, in great peace, while peace most humble, recollecting this truth, into the "changes and chances of this mortal life." No two days and hours are quite alike; no two hearts and lives. On this we have already dwelt, as we considered* the manifoldness of need. But here is the heavenly antidote to the trials of *succession*, as we saw it above to the trials of *multiplicity*. For the succession in us there is this divine succession in our Lord. For the struggles of yesterday He was present with the needed fulness. That fulness is not attenuated by the "out going" of the "virtue" then; for it comes to us in this unwearying exchange and newness. It is full, in the same channel but a new flood, for the struggles of to-day. And to-morrow it shall be the same.

What is your special need? Is it some

* Ch. VII.

great sorrow of *loss*—loss of strength, of wealth, of affection, of beloved ones who lighted up your life? Is it some great problem of action, duty new and momentous, accumulations of demand upon your narrow hours? Is it the perplexity of wandering thoughts in the hour of hearing God's Word, or of prayer? Is it some other need altogether internal, defilements in the inmost world of imagination and desire, stirrings of corruption far within? Is it need markedly external, temptation to principle, to patience, coming upon you from without? Is it the agonies of perplexity* about some mystery of the

* How different are such pains from the unhappy complacency of a mind vain of its doubts, or proud in them! When Asaph (Psal. lxxiii.) was brought to rest, by the simplest looking off to God, he did not say, "How intellectual I am!" but "So foolish was I, and ignorant." But what a dire conflict it was while it lasted, before he bethought him of carrying it into "the sanctuary"!

Word and Ways of God? Is it the need implied in a life of toil, or that which comes with leisure, the solemn trust of hours with which you "may do what you will"? Is it pangs of memory, or of anticipation—present griefs, though not caused by the present? Of the pangs of memory, is it one of the worst—recollection of a time when a peace and joy in Jesus Christ were yours which are not yours to-day? Of the pangs of anticipation is it one of the most wearing—expectation of future failure in your life and service for your Lord?

It is need for need, weakness for weakness. Yes, but behold also grace for grace; not for yesterday, but for to-day; and for to-morrow when to-morrow is to-day. Be sure of this, that your Lord and Life will never, no, not for an hour, or for a minute, leave you with an inadequate supply of "Himself working in you, Phil. ii. 13.

to will and to do"—to begin again, or to go on again, willing and doing—"for His good pleasure's sake."

Do not fear the certainty of perpetual needs. Do not fear the fact that the Enemy will attempt you to the last, and
Rom. vii. 18. that to the last "in your flesh" will "dwell no good thing." Do not be disheartened by the longest retrospect of failures. Look, and see for this moment the moment's divine succession of supply in Jesus Christ. And be perfectly sure that neither for this moment nor any other is there "fulness" anywhere else.

I have quoted at the head of the chapter those words of the Psalmist which lead us up the River to its Source. "For with Thee is the fountain of Life"; with Thee, JEHOVAH; with Thee, JEHOVAH-CHRIST,
1 Joh. v. 11, 12. for "in Thee is Life"; "he that hath Thee hath life."

Let that verse just remind us of the

duty and the blessing of continual remembrance of Him as our reason and our rest. There is such a thing as studying even the "possibilities of grace" more than Him who is "the God of all grace." 1 Pet. v. 10.

It is because of what He is that His people are, even for a moment, what He would have them be. And one deep secret of the development in them of what He would have there, is the contemplation of Him. 2 Cor. iii. 18.

Our life and walk, in a sense most practical, need be no intermittent stream of peace and of obedience. Why? Because He is no intermittent spring. Every winter, in modern Jerusalem, a remarkable phenomenon is observed. The channel of the Kedron, usually dry as the valley of dry bones, suddenly resounds with the music of waters. Whatever be the natural cause hidden in the geology of the ravine, for some four or five days the

Kedron suddenly and abundantly springs and flows; or, to speak more exactly, it begins abundantly, shrinks somewhat on the second day, and ere long, failing day by day, it has retired into the dry rocks again. Strange and pathetic intermittency! True picture and parable of too many a Christian life and experience! But need it be? "For with Him is the fountain of Life";
Cant. iv. 12. "a spring shut up, a fountain sealed" (if we may borrow words of the Holy Song, though they are spoken directly not of Him but of His Bride); shut up, and sealed,
Zech. xiii. i. as to all access outside of Him; but "a fountain opened," not only for pardon, but for life and power, to all who are in Him.

Isai. lv. 1. Come then, let us come now and ever, to the waters. The eternal Rock is smitten, and is flowing; and where? In the desert, in the drought; to turn the sands into the oasis; to make "the wil-
Isai. xxxv. 1, 7. derness and the solitary place glad" now.

It is written of the everlasting Canaan that "they shall thirst no more, for the Lamb shall shepherd them, and lead them to the living fountains of waters." But it is also written of the pathway thither, that "they shall not thirst, for He that hath mercy on them shall lead them, even by the springs of water shall He guide them." Let us ask Him to do it indeed. Then we "shall not be careful in the year of drought, nor cease from yielding fruit."

Rev. vi 16, 17.

Isai. xlix. 10.

Jer. xvii. 8.

IX.

LIVING WATER.

THE last chapter was full of thoughts of the River and the Well. Let us linger a while longer in the same region of
Deut. viii. 7. Scriptural imagery; it is a region full "of fountains and depths, that spring out of valleys and hills."

The words "living water" occur in two remarkable passages of St John's Gospel, passages widely separated in time and circumstance, but closely united in spiritual significance by this phrase, and that, too, in a way which makes the second passage the true sequel and development of the first.

In ch. iv. 14, the Lord Jesus tells the

woman of Sychar that had she known the gift of God, and known Him who spoke to her, she would have asked, and He would have given living water; and that this water would have precluded all thirst for ever; and that it would prove to be, within its recipient, a fountain of water, of water not stagnant but "springing, leaping, unto eternal life."

And in ch. vii. 38, we hear the same Voice speak of living water in a far different scene. Not seated alone with one listener by the rural well, but standing in the midst of the crowds and movement of the great day of a great Temple festival, He invites all who thirst to "come to Him,
and drink." And by this He means "to ver. 39.
believe on Him." And He assures His hearers that as this is done the result shall be not merely a reception of living water, but such a reception as shall be an overflow. Out of the drinker, out of the

believer, "shall flow rivers of living water. And this spake He of the Spirit, which they that believed on Him should receive."

In the occasions and contexts of each of these utterances there is indeed much to study. The very contrast, to which I have already alluded, between the extreme difference of the two sets of circumstances and the holy sameness of the Lord's thought and tone amidst them, would alone be matter for fruitful meditation. It is full of illustration of what HE was and is. It is full of example for His followers. And let us never forget that the example of Christ is, for His followers, the example of Him with whom they are vitally and indissolubly one.

But these thoughts are not my main purpose at present. Nor do I attempt even a brief comment on all the details of the two utterances themselves. I ask my reader's attention now for only two or three main points. Let us think of the sacred Gift itself; and of its personal possession by the believer in Christ; and of its conveyance through him to others.

i. The Gift; the Living Water. St John, that is to say, the Holy Spirit by him, explains this to mean the Holy Spirit. It is the personal Paraclete. And it is the Paraclete in a mode of presence and action specially conditioned by the soul's having come to Christ, having believed on Christ, already. True it is, deeply true, that when we come and believe it is already because of the Spirit, the Spirit of Faith. But this is not the phase of truth before us in these two utterances. The Lord takes the case of the man as having, anyhow, come and believed. Then, in the sense of after-experience, after-life, in manifestation, unfolding, indwelling, empowering, the man shall "receive the

2 Cor. iv. 13.

Spirit." In a sense different from that which might have been true before, the Spirit, the Holy Ghost, shall be in him, and he in the Spirit. He shall be a
1 Cor. ii. 15. "spiritual" man, not in any vague sense, not merely as having, somehow, a higher range of interests and ideas. He shall be, in a sense as literal as it is divine, actuated by the development of a new Life, the Life Eternal, the Life of the Head of the newborn Race, the Life imparted, maintained, dilated, by nothing less than the personal presence in his very being of the Holy Spirit, the divine Agent alike of the Human Birth of the Head and of the New Birth of each Limb.

The Spirit shall be in that man, in this
Eph iii. 17. sense, and therefore "Christ shall dwell in his heart." I lay stress on this last point, because of its extreme practical importance in the whole subject of the life of faith and peace. Let us remember on the one

hand that we possess the Lord's indwelling by the Holy Spirit only. Let us remember on the other hand that what we possess by the Holy Spirit is above all things the indwelling Lord. We are not to look for two separate experiences, so to speak; a presence of the Spirit and a presence of Christ. The presence of Christ is thanks to the blessed Spirit's presence. The Spirit's presence is to be known—how? By the character of our actual relations of thought, love, and will with Christ; by our view of His unsearchable preciousness, by our rest in His dominion, by our peaceful power over self and sin in Him. To receive the living water is to be filled, or, however, to be filling, with Him, revealed and applied by the Spirit.

This then, let us remember, is the promised, the guaranteed, gift of God in Christ to all, to all who come.

ii. Now turn to the promise of the Well. Its main concern is with the personal possession of this Gift; not yet with its liberation, so to speak, and distribution through the possessor. The Lord undertakes that the man who drinks that water shall never thirst; obviously in the sense of never needing to seek for other wells, and of never needing to complain of an intermittent supply from *this* well. He shall find that he has received the ultimate answer to his entire need. He shall find that he has so received it that he may, if he will, be always enjoying it, always resting in it, always living in it.

To follow the precise words further, the water which Christ shall give him, the water which he shall owe to the work and love of Christ, "shall become (so literally) in him a spring of water, of water leaping up, unto eternal life."

I do not examine minutely those

last three words. It is interesting to ask whether they mean, "until the arrival of the state of glory, the ultimate phase of eternal life," or whether they may not rather mean, "unto, resulting evermore in, the present realities and experiences of eternal life"; in other words, "so as to underlie, secure, and blessedly convey, the life of God in Christ evermore to the needs and longings of the man." But it is not material now to discuss this.

What is material is the assurance that "the water shall become in him a spring of up-leaping water." Here we have, for one thing, the delightful assurance (let us treat it as an assurance) that the holy Thing shall be *in* the man. The context shews that the special point of the thought here is that he shall carry it about with him, in the depth of his being, always and everywhere. He shall not need to travel, or to toil, to get it within him. In his travelling and in his toiling it shall be within him. Go where he may, do, bear, what he may, meet whatever he may at any time by way of circumstances, he shall not be dependent for a moment upon circumstances for his water of life. It is his by gift. It is in him always, in him now. Alone with self and the Tempter, he bears it in him. Deep in the stress and throng of life, it is in him. In his strongest hour, and in his weakest, this holy Thing, which is not himself but the Spirit, and Christ by the Spirit, is in him.

Then further observe the phrase, "it shall *become* a spring of up-leaping water." Is it not as much as to say that the Gift as realized, and watched, and used, shall develope its true character and preciousness? It might be suspected at first to be but a cup; it shall soon prove to be a source, a spring, a depth originating in God.

It shall be not only always there, but always new there, while always the same there. The happy possessor of it shall be always antecedently supplied for all circumstances, in this experience and discovery that the water is a spring. And thus he shall be independent of circumstances, in a sense very real and happy. He will be no despiser of "means of grace;" nay, he will prize them in their right use more than ever. But they will be to him means of cultivation and advance in the knowledge and the use of grace far rather than supposed originations of it. His water-spring is within him, always within him.

And it proves to be a spring of water "leaping up." The imagery is beautifully special. The immortal supply is from an ultimate Source so living that its flow has not motion only but a motion of gentle while vivid life. The idea conveyed is that of "the Spirit's calm excess," in the

beautiful words of an ancient hymn. The soul's experience shall have about it a chastened life and brightness through Him who thus divinely dwells within. Joy, in the pure depth of that word in the spiritual vocabulary, joy hall pervade the being. The certainties of grace, of the Spirit, of Christ, shall give to the soul a commentary all their own on the apostolic word,
2 Cor. vi. 10. "always rejoicing." Yes, there shall be that humble but profound pleasure, which we have studied above,* pleasure even in
2 Cor. xii. 9. distresses, in infirmities, "that the power of Christ may overshadow us."

Such is the matter as it stands in the personal and definite promise of the Lord at the Well. Let me take it, let me remind my reader to take it, in its holy
2 Cor vii. 1. simplicity and fulness. And "having this promise, let us cleanse ourselves." Let us do our practical part by seeing to it, in

* Ch. V.

watching and prayer, that the weeds and rubbish are cleared from the basin of the spring, and that no stone lies needlessly upon its mouth.

iii. Now for a few moments let us pass on to the Temple cloister, to the Lord's utterance on the great day of the feast. Here is the living water again, and the coming, and the receiving. And here is this development of the promise; there shall be an overflow. I say nothing on the place of the quotation; "as the Scripture hath said." Enough for us now that Christ, in *this* Scripture, hath said it.

What does it mean? It means that the man who really drinks of Christ, drinking of the Spirit, shall assuredly be a conveyer, a conductor, for the Spirit, for Christ, to others. It means that the really and livingly spiritual man shall be a spiritual blessing, a spiritual power. The thought requires, of course, a reverent

caution. It cannot mean that he shall be an origin of grace; and indeed this is guarded by the special imagery, in which the thought is fixed on the drinking the Spirit from Christ, and no mention is made of the spring within, which might have seemed possibly to countenance the notion of our becoming origins, though it would not have done so really. Nor again is there any assurance here that at our own will or decision we can convey blessing to others. That is the express prerogative of the Lord Himself. But the assurance is that we shall be richly fruitful, somehow, of spiritual results; of results in others in the way of their also tasting of the gift of God. Our work in the matter is to drink, is to believe; to
Gal. ii. 20. live by faith on the Son of God, who obeyed and died for us and liveth in us. His undertaking is that we shall be, in proportion, aqueducts for His living water.

More is meant here, surely, than that we shall merely know what to say, and say it. This is something indeed; this is a great thing. But it is a thing in which a hypocrite can be a conductor. The truth here is that He will use the man, or the woman, who is really drinking the heavenly Water from the Rock, who is really filled for life's need with the supplies of life eternal, in another, a more mysterious way, and yet a way all the while profoundly natural. Through that personality the Spirit shall be pleased to work special blessings, for He will have made it fit to be so used. It shall livingly reflect something of the glory of the Lord. It shall be a true channel of persuasion, attraction, conviction. It "shall be a vessel unto honour, sanctified, serviceable to the Master." The believer in question may perhaps *know* that he is thus privileged and employed, by manifest results of fact; he may conspicu- 2 Tim. ii. 21.

ously be "a blessing" to very many souls and lives around him. Or he may never know it thus at all. But that matters, comparatively, little. The concern is with the Master's knowledge, the Master's interests, not the servant's. For the servant, for the bondservant, let it be enough to know that the Master meant what He said, and will be found to have kept His word, to His own glory.

X.

CHRISTIAN SERVICE.

This chapter reproduces a written Address prepared for a public occasion. It has been left on purpose nearly as it originally stood.

CHRISTIAN Service, in its full idea, is a phrase practically coextensive with Christian life; and Christian life is, in the intention of the Gospel, nothing less, nothing narrower, than the whole life of the Christian; morning, noon, and night; alone, in private, in society, in public; at all times and in all places. From one point of view, and that a most important point, he not only is a servant of the Lord, but he is a servant of the Lord in such a way, under such conditions, that

the whole action of his life falls under the description of service. As he always exists, as a Christian, in and by his Master, so he always exists for his Master. He has, in the reality of the matter, no dissociated and independent interest. Not only in preaching and teaching, and bearing articulate witness to Jesus Christ, does he, if his life is true to its idea and its
Rom. xiv. 7. secret, "live not unto himself"; not with aims which terminate for one moment in his own credit, for example, or his own comfort. Equally in the engagements of domestic life, of business life, of public affairs; equally (to look towards the humbler walks of duty) in the day's work of the Christian servant, or peasant,
Rom. xiv. 8 or artizan; "whether he lives, he lives unto the Master, or whether he dies, he dies unto the Master"; whether he wakes or sleeps, whether he toils or rests, whether it be the term or the vacation of life,

"whether he eats or drinks, or whatsoever he does," he is the Master's property for the Master's use. 1 Cor. x. 31.

"Teach me, my God and King,
In all things Thee to see,
And what I do in anything
To do it as to Thee.

"A servant with this clause
Makes drudgery divine;
Who sweeps a room as for Thy laws
Makes that and th' action fine."

So wrote Herbert, two centuries and a half ago. And the Gospel principle is immoveably the same for us to-day. Let us not content ourselves even for a moment, in view of it, with the all too easy piety of an abstract assent and indefinite aspiration. Looking afresh, looking with adoring steadiness, at our beloved Lord, let us embrace in humblest practicality the all-inclusive conditions of His service.

Rom. vi. 13. In His name, in His presence, let us yield to Him ourselves, as those who are already alive from the dead through Him. The probable result in our life will be no startling exterior revolution, but a happy and wonderful increase, as we go forward, of quietness, and preparedness, and liberty within. "His service," in precise proportion to the simplicity and entirety of our acceptance of its bond and yoke, "is perfect freedom." *Illi servire est regnare*; and let us remember that *servire* means bondservice; the service in which not only certain functions and acquirements of mine are hired out under conditions to another, but in which another has taken absolute possession of me.

Such, briefly indicated, is Christian Service. It is for all always. And the conditions to its true exercise are the same for all; a walk with God in the secret of the soul; a renunciation of all thought of intermittency in the service; a simple and expectant reliance on the heavenly Master's will to accept it and power to use it.

For our present purpose, however, we will consider Christian Service under a limitation. We will think of it as meaning the service rendered by any of the great multitude of "Christian workers" as such. It may be the service of the commissioned pastor of the flock; it may be that of the visitor of the sick, of the rescuer of the fallen, of the teacher of the Bible class or the Sunday school, of the lay worker in mission-room or open air. It may be any one who seeks definitely to influence others for Christ.

If such is service, what then are the qualifications for it, or, more properly, some of the chief things amongst them?

One word, if but in passing, let me say as to the message which the servant of

Christ carries. There is urgent need for the Christian worker of our day to take care of his personal hold upon articulate, fundamental truth, as well as over his spirit of zeal and love. Zeal is not enough, nor energy, nor willingness to endure much hardness. All these things can, as a
Gal. i. 6 7. matter of experience, go along with "another Gospel, which is not another." There must be humble and laborious pains about the Scriptural solidity and rightness of the message, as well as about the energy of the messenger.

But I turn now to the personal rather than to the doctrinal qualifications of the servant of the Lord. And here first: would the worker be what the Master would have him be as a worker? Then let him be a consistent man all round. Would he serve in testimony? Then let him serve in everything. Would he be influential for his Master's sake, far and wide, if a broad field of influence is, as a fact, open to him? Then let his wife, his children, his parents, his whole home circle, his circle of acquaintance, business, or labour, find him out as a servant of Jesus Christ in all ways that practically touch them.

I recently heard, with much interest, a remark on the religion of English Church people made to a friend of mine by a member of the Church of the *Unitas Fratrum*, commonly called the Moravian Church, in Germany. "Your preachings," said the Moravian, "are often admirable, far beyond much that we say or hear. Your statements of doctrine, your testimonies to Christ, and to His grace and power, are full and beautiful But we see, as a rule, a great difference between your preachings and your lives. We, perhaps, have a humbler aim in the pulpit, but we seek to live all that we preach." And my friend spoke with loving admiration of what the consistency of Moravian life was; above all, in its being pervaded everywhere and in all things, to an extent deeply impressive, and strongly attractive, with humility of heart, and with peace and joy in the Lord.

Let our inference for ourselves, from such a comparison, be in favour not of a lower doctrine, or a more misgiving testimony, but of a bringing into real practice what in theory we know so well. Let us settle it in our inmost convictions that the life of the disciple is intended to be one, and of a piece; and that his work detail stands related, certainly from his Lord's point of view, in a profound and vital connexion, to his habits, his temper, his manner of life in general. Consistency
2 Tim. 21. is indissolubly bound up with "meetness for the Master's use."

To turn to another point, which is, after all, but one point of special brightness in the bright circle of consistency. I refer to that great qualification for Christian Service on which we have already dwelt in a previous chapter—an honest and unaffected self-forgetfulness, let me call it selflessness, in the worker's soul, with reference to the work.

Deep in our nature, in the Fall, lies the sin of which this is the blessed contrary; and alas for the manifestations of that sin in the circles of Christian service! It appears all too often in just the most energetic, the most versatile, the most clever, of the servants of Christ those, perhaps, gifted with most capacity to originate and direct. Their capacities are the Master's golden talents, and are certainly meant to be employed, in His time. But then, as the solemn associations of the misused word *talent* should of themselves remind us, they are never, no not for an hour, to be used for self, but for Him. The eager thought that the work, the enterprise, the organization, the connexion, is *mine*, is to be kept in jealous check. The first symptoms of religious envy are to be by the Lord's servant as promptly and thoroughly dealt with as would be those of a formidable bodily disease; or rather, what is far better, the servant is to remember beforehand the danger of infection, and to live therefore in that germ-killing air, the presence and the peace of God.

It is a sorrowful sight, but not a very rare one, to see some otherwise admirable Christian ill of this disease already, and not taking the least action against it; to see a man manifestly equipped with manifold powers, and skill to use them, but with whom one fellow-worker after another "finds it very hard to work."

For the Christian in question is not content with being *qualified* to be first, to lead, to be prominent; he cannot be happy in any second place.

And it is scarcely needful to point out that the exciting causes of this malady can arise not only from the individual, but from the individual's circle, whether it be the circle of personal connexion, or of special line of Christian enterprise, or of ecclesiastical organization. It is one thing to be loyal to well-loved associates and colleagues, to be soberly convinced about certain principles of Church order. It is quite another thing, and, alas, it is far more common and more easy, I fear, to be simply prejudiced, and filled with the spirit of self, in regard, for instance, of some marked blessing sent down on work or workers going upon a different, not to say an alien, line. But this spirit is from beneath, not from above. It has no necessary connexion whatever with fixity of principle, clearness of conviction, and a discernment of things that differ. Analyse it, and it will come out as the spirit of self, the precise antithesis to the spirit of the Gospel. Let us, for our life of service, live habitually in the holy air in which this cannot live.

This leads me to say a little, in closing, of the all-importance to the servant of Jesus Christ of the maintenance of his own personal joy and glory in his Master. The sad secret of the spirit I have just sought to deprecate lies in the subtle substitution, somewhere and somehow, of self for Jesus Christ. It is calling the work "mine" instead of "His." It is working for my credit rather than for His glory. It is attracting, or trying to attract, to me, not altogether to Him. And where shall we go for the remedy? It must be to Him. It must be found in the renewal of our sight of Him, without one cloud between, even the cloud of our own restless activities. We must get a new view of "the fair beauty of the Lord," and of the blessedness and pleasantness of our lot and part in Him. Psal. xxvii. 4, Prayer Book.

"From the loss of our glory in Thee, preserve and keep us, gracious Lord and God." Such is one response in a solemn Litany of that venerable Moravian Church to which I referred just now.

I have read of a servant of Christ in the past, a man singularly rich in the gift of spiritual influence over individuals. He was asked to disclose something of his secret. His reply, in essence, was tha it lay, as far as he knew, in the sense of profound contentment with his blessed Master in which his soul was kept through grace. Jesus Christ irradiated him within and for himself. He was, at the very centre of his soul's consciousness, deeply happy to belong to "his

King who had saved him," and to be used by that great and holy Possessor as should seem best to Him. And this took friction and anxiety out of his life in a very wonderful way, while it kept that life, so to speak, always directed, peacefully and unwearily, towards the thought of service, towards the idea, and the expectation, of being used. And the service was all the happier, because it was not the source of the man's happiness. The source and secret was Jesus Christ; and that secret acted equally whether marked success attended action and speech, or apparently no success at all; whether the servant was put by the Master into the front rank of active reapers in the harvest field, or told to "sit down in a corner and sharpen the sickles of others"; whether he was called to speak in spiritual power to a multitude, or to lie still on a sick bed. That heaven-given spirit, in a blessed

paradox, was for him the source at once of workfulness and of repose. And in a very marked degree it preserved the worker from the infection of the sin of envy, of jealousy, of selfishness. Ah! in the air of a life so hid with Christ in God, do we not feel instinctively that such sin could not breathe? "The fruit of right- Jas. iii. 18.
eousness is sown in peace"; in the peace of God. It is one of the deepest and most sacred laws of the life of the children of God that their activity has its root in passivity; their strength has profoundly much to do with weakness; their rising up and going on with giving way and sinking down; with that opposite of positive effort which is yet so fruitful of work—"Yield yourselves unto God." Rom. vi. 13.

"From the loss of our glory in Thee, preserve and keep us—us who humbly ask to serve Thee for ever—gracious Lord and God."

In immediate conclusion, I would most earnestly plead, then, in the interests of true Christian service, for what in these hurrying times we need so specially: a deeper entrance of our souls into the secret of the presence of the Lord. Work is not food for the spirit any more than for the body. Amidst a multitude of works the worker's soul may wither, and the works will feel the difference in due time. We must, because we are servants and not masters, bondservants and not contractors, limbs and not Head, we must see to it that we are living and serving not only so as to get through a great deal of action, but so as to be vessels meet for the Master's use, in His way and not our own. And for this we must live, so to speak, behind our service; we must live, in a true and holy sense, independent of it. We must live upon Jesus Christ, not upon energy, upon success, upon notice, upon praise; God forbid.

And to live upon Him in service, we must, in the rule and habit of our lives, watch over times of solemn, sacred, blessed intercourse with Him in secret. We must, despite all the influences of our day, make time for thoughtful prayer, for reverent search into His Word, for re-collection of our treasures in Him, time to exercise the more deliberate acts of a living faith in His great promises, and in the unseen realities of the things eternal. So shall we come forth evermore to serve, and to serve indeed.

Thank God, the picture is not a visionary one—not an ideal of the land of the clouds. It is the secret of many a life of steadfast, chastened, humble, Christ-reflecting service in the great Church of God to-day. And the Lord, in whom that open secret lies, can make it for all His servants their own happy possession. So shall it be for us, by His grace, to His glory. Amen.

XI.

CONCLUDING THOUGHTS.

In closing these simple pages, let me put before my friend and reader a few remarks, somewhat detached in form.

i. First, an earnest caution against an overdrawn *introspection.* It may be thought that this book itself looks another way, often suggesting and encouraging a close inward examination. I do indeed seek to press, on myself first, the duty of self-examination, a scrutiny within that shall not stop short of motive, purpose, inmost state of affection and will. Many Christian lives, I am sure, greatly lose in depth, consistency, and chastened oberness, by the failure to examine within; and the habit and practice of such examination, not without a certain system, is a duty of Christian life. For most of us it would be well to make this exercise a regular element, say, in secret evening devotion.

Nevertheless, introspection is a secondary, not primary, duty of the life of
grace; a subsidiary, not direct, means of
holiness and strength. "Ten looks at
Christ for one at self" is after all the
primary rule. "Look unto Jesus" gives Heb. xii.
us, as has been well said, the Gospel 2.
in three words. Introspection ceases to
do good and begins to do harm the moment it terminates in itself, the moment
it fails to be our reminder of our need of
the simplest gaze, every hour, upon the
Son of God, "who is made unto us of God 1 Cor.
wisdom, and righteousness, and sanctifica- i. 30.
tion, and redemption." Christ is "the
Secret of God," in the literal rendering of

the best attested reading of Col. ii. 2. And
Christ is not ourselves. Dwelling in the
Eph. iii. 16. heart of him who is "strengthened by the
Spirit in the inner man," He is not the
inner man, nor the heart. And, as *the
Object of adoring contemplation and humble
faith*, we must view Him not as He is
in us but as He is in Himself; incar-
2 Cor. iii. 18. nate, sacrificed, glorified. "Beholding
the glory of the Lord, we are changed
into the same image, as by the Lord the
Spirit."

ii. As one part of this general subject,
I lay it upon myself and my reader, as we
seek to live day by day in the strength of
the risen Jesus Christ, all the more to lean
our *acceptance* before God wholly, solely,
upon the finished Work of our redeeming
Jer. xxiii. 6. Sacrifice, "the Lord our Righteousness."
The holy thirst and hunger to please
God is a radically different thing from the
anxious effort to reconcile God. Blessed

be His name, that work is done, is completed, for us, by the obedience of One. Rom. v. 19.
In the deep words of the Second Article, "Christ, very God and very man, truly suffered, was crucified, dead, and buried, to reconcile His Father to us, and to be a sacrifice not only for original guilt but also for all actual sins of men." And in the words of the Eleventh, never to be separated from those others, "We are accounted righteous before God, ONLY for the merit of our Lord and Saviour Jesus Christ, by faith (*per fidem*)." Such words, technical as they may sound, speak a truth inexpressibly restful to the fully awakened conscience. Do you see the depth of the demand of God's law? Do you believe what His Word says, speaking, remember, in the person of an inspired saint, "Enter Psal. cxliii. 2
not into judgment with Thy servant, O Lord; for in Thy sight shall no man living be justified"? Do you see the sin

(to speak of nothing else) of the least inadequacy in your love to God, in your love to others? Then, in true proportion to the spiritual reality and fulness of such insight, you will prize, you will adore, you will submit yourself to, you will lean yourself upon, the finished Satisfaction, the imputed Merit, of your Redeemer. In the words of a departed saint, to whose soul the truth of saving love in this aspect was singularly real and sweet, you will rejoice to feel that "the bed is large enough to lie down upon, the covering ample enough to wrap round" the awakened soul.

iii. In the practice of daily life, in the derivation from the risen Lord of the power of "new obedience," let me and my reader recollect steadily, and weave into one cord — a cord that at once binds and knits—two sacred facts of our state as believers. First, we BELONG to the Lord; secondly, we are JOINED to Him.

"Whether we live, we live unto the Master; whether we die, we die unto the Master." Let the words "I BELONG" be written, in redeeming blood, across your whole life. Wake up with that fact in recollection; not that feeling but that fact. Carry it into morning, noon, and night. Lie down upon your bed with it. We have dwelt on this side of truth already, elsewhere.* But let it be pressed home on heart and will once more. Everything else tends to fall abroad and into pieces without it. Nature fears it, but when by the grace of God a man has looked it in the face, or far rather has looked in the face THE MASTER who makes the claim, it is peace and rest to surrender, quite at discretion, to that Ownership. "To this end," that

Rom. xiv 8.

Rom. xiv. 9.

* In the author's "Thoughts on Christian Sanctity," ch. iv.

He might be Master, "He died and rose again." This must be, this is, a very blessed "end"—for Possessor and possessed!

> "I love, I love my Master; I will not go out free;
> For He is my Redeemer; He paid the price for me."

Happy, happy, the human will that is bound with this chain. It is free indeed. Make proof, on the Master's warrant, and "thou shalt know."

1 Cor. vi. 17. But again, we are "JOINED to the Lord," So says the Spirit. The passage and context are full of the essence of the new Life and its exercise. We gather there, that the believer belongs to Christ not merely as a man's watch, for instance, but as his hand, belongs to him. And observe that this is true for *every* "limb" of the blessed Head; not for the highly developed member only, but for the member; yes, as the whole passage shows, even for the

member struggling with the force of the crudest and basest temptation. For the disheartened, aye, for the falling Christian, this word is written: "you are joined to the Lord" now; you are "one Spirit" now. It is not reward of obedience, but gift of God. The word is not "you ought," but "you possess." It is not "you feel it," but "thus it is." What have you, thus united, to do with sin? What need temptation do against you, thus united?

The man who recollects his belongingness to Jesus Christ, his irrevocable lot and state of bondservice to Him, and who recollects *along with it* his living union with Him, is the man who may humbly, calmly, and with restful expectation say with St Paul, "I can do all things in Him that strengtheneth me." Phil. iv. 13.
"Nothing shall in any wise hurt him." Luke x. 19.
Shall we take our place, in the name of

the Lord Jesus, among these people, and go forward in this blessed double recollection, not into some imagined path of duty and patience, but into our own?

Very real, very great, is the power and preciousness of the holy Supper of the Lord, in the light of this combination of truths. Our redemption to be the property of our beloved Saviour, and our mystical Union with Him as our Head, are there, in the same divine act, "visibly signed and sealed" by HIMSELF, the true Master of the Table, to each true disciple. What certainties of assurance, what warrants of strength and peace, lie in that fact!

iv. And one remark let me make here on
2 Tim. iii. 15; iv. 2. the study of the Scriptures, which are the Word of God. On the duty, privilege, and method, I am not going to enlarge. It is in special connexion with the life of Christian Holiness, the life of new Obedience, that I speak of Scripture study; and specially

in view of the fact that Scripture is the one *articulate* account, by the Lord Himself, of His "will in Jesus Christ concerning us." For you, believing friend, who long to know and to do His will, as at once your rest and your goal, let the Bible bear *this* aspect of sacredness very specially, that it is the one definite and articulate utterance of that Will by our Master Himself. From this point of view how singular is the value of the hundred and nineteenth Psalm! It has been beautifully said that the essence of the thought of that Psalm is, the sacredness and sweetness of God's Will, to be known and done by His bondservant; so that we may reverently read, as it were, the word "will" into it, as a synonym for "law," "statutes," "judgments," "precepts," &c. Try this holy gloss, and see how the verses shine with the glory of a loving surrender to the will of God. But then, on the other hand, beyond all question, the Psalm in its direct

1 Thess. v. 18.

purpose is one long strain of prayer, and praise, and self-consecration, *over the Bible.* The saintly soul's thirst after the will of God leads it not to the mirage, but to the water-spring of the Word. With every access of love and longing, with every step in conscience and obedience, he feels new need of the Book, he bends over it, he bows to it. So be it with you and with me.

v. Lastly, and let this reflection touch
Eph. v. 2; and attune every other, let us "walk in
1 Joh. iv. 7 love, for love is of God." Even the few pages of this little book, dealing with topics of the inner life, have led me to definite statements of conviction on many points of truth and doctrine. My whole soul is sure of the importance of clearness and firmness in such things. Nevertheless, there is no region of Christian life in which the need is more constant and more strong to remember how to walk in

love, than the doctrinal region. It is easy, very easy, as we have observed more than once already, to disguise to ourselves a jealousy for our own views *as such* under an aspect of jealousy for the revealed truth of God. There lies the danger; there lies the need. And the remedy, the supply, lies above all things in a deepening personal acquaintance with "the Son of God, who loved me and gave Himself for me." Gal. ii. 20.

In the divine serenity of His presence we can, so far as our personality and sensibility go, read in peace the page from which we differ, perhaps the page which takes ourselves severely to task, and can ask in peace and candour where lies the truth. Walking by the side of Jesus Christ, we can with joy and love see His image reflected in the life and labour of the Christian man with whom, perhaps on no unimportant point, we are at issue.

Psal. lxi. 4. "In the covert of His wings" we can love, as well as watch. Ambitious and jealous not for ourselves but for Him whose property we are, we shall find more attraction in the least sign of genuine loyalty to Him than we can find repulsion in almost anything else. For this also His grace is sufficient.

Our series of thoughts is over. To that Master of Whom we have just spoken—absolute, merciful, beloved—I now humbly commit the things written. Whatever among them are indeed "the things of Christ," He can bless, forgiving the rest. And for us, writer and reader, "the next thing" shall be to step forward into the realities of to-day, putting thought into practice, seeing in circumstances God's will, receiving amidst them His Spirit, living through them upon Jesus Christ, who is our Life. To Him be glory, now and always. Amen.

"Certainly, the more the Christian is acquainted with himself, the more will he go out of himself for his perfecting and establishing. . . . . Never shall we find heart peace, sweet peace, and progress in holiness, till we be driven from natural independency, to make Christ all our strength; till we be brought to do nothing, to attempt nothing, to hope or expect nothing, but in Him; and then shall we indeed find His fulness and all-sufficiency, and 'be more than conquerors through Him who hath loved us.'"

Archbishop Leighton, on 1 Pet. v. 10.

HYMNS.

"He shall receive of mine, and shall shew it unto you."—Joh. xvi. 14.

Come, Holy Comforter, celestial Light,
Relieve from all obscurity our sight;
Come, Holy Comforter, celestial Fire,
Our souls with love and purity inspire;
Hear, Holy Ghost, our supplicating cry,
Nor leave the grace Thou gav'st to droop
and die!

Come, Holy Comforter, the Saviour's love
Reveal, and fix our hearts on joys above;
Come, Holy Comforter, the flesh subdue,
And aid us, one with Christ, His will to
do;
Hear, Holy Ghost, our supplicating cry,
Nor leave the grace Thou gav'st to droop
and die!

Henry Moule, 1846.

"Thy will be done."—Matt. vi. 10.

Our Father, to that heavenly Home,
Beyond this high cerulean dome,
No rebel will nor deed can come;—
Thy Will is done.

Thou willest that each heart shall glow
With rapturous willingness to go
On Thy blest messages—and lo,
Thy Will is done.

Thou willest that no wing shall tire,
Never burn low Love's sacred fire,
Nor cease the full melodious choir;
Thy Will is done.

Oh glorious Will, oh strength of Love,
By which the Blessed ceaseless move!
On earth, as it is done above,
Thy Will be done!

My God, my Father, see Thy child
Threading in grief earth's sinful wild:
Thou will'st me trustful, undefiled;[1]
Thy Will be done!

'Tis not Thy Will (I heard Thee say)
That I should be a castaway,[2]
But rise in glory[3];—so I pray,
Thy Will be done!

Wilt Thou have all men to be saved,[4]
And free all souls by sin enslaved?[5]
Thy chariot-floor with love is paved;[6]
Thy Will be done!

All crowns shall glitter on His brow
Who gave for me His blood to flow;
To Jesus every knee shall bow;[7]
Thy Will be done!

[1] Phil. ii. 13–15.
[2] Matt. xviii. 14. [3] Joh. vi. 39.
[4] 1 Tim. ii. 4, 6. [5] Joh. v. 40.
[6] Cant. iii. 10.
[7] Isai. xlv. 23; Rom. xiv. 10, 11; Phil. ii. 10.

All that my will can never choose,—
Sin's burthen,—He did not refuse;
The sweet I gain, the bitter lose:
Thy Will be done!

My Father, Master, Lord, fulfil
In me the filial likeness, till
I say, when Thou hast freed MY will,
THY Will be done!

A. E. MOULE, B.D.

Ningpo, 1875.

From "Songs of Heaven and Home."

"I will come in to him."—Rev. iii. 20.

Come in, O come! The door stands open now;
I knew Thy voice; Lord Jesus, it was Thou;
The sun has set long since; the storms begin;
'Tis time for Thee, my Saviour; O come in!

Come, even now. But think not here to find
A lodging, Lord, and converse, to Thy mind:
The lamp burns low; the hearth is chill and pale;
Wet through the broken casement pours the gale.

Alas, ill-order'd shews the dreary room;
The household-stuff lies heap'd amidst the gloom;
The table empty stands, the couch undress'd;
Ah, what a welcome for the Eternal Guest!

Yet welcome, and to-night; this doleful scene
Is e'en itself my cause to hail Thee in;
This dark confusion e'en at once demands
Thine own bright presence, Lord, and ordering hands.

I seek no more to alter things, or mend,
Before the coming of so great a Friend:
All were at best unseemly; and 't were ill
Beyond all else to keep Thee waiting still.

Then, as Thou art, all holiness and bliss,
Come in, and see my chamber as it is;
I bid Thee welcome boldly, in the name
Of Thy great glory and my want and shame.

Come, not to find, but make, this troubled heart
A dwelling worthy of Thee as Thou art;
To chase the gloom, the terror, and the sin,
Come, all Thyself, yea come, Lord Jesus, in!

H. C. G. M.

"Your life is hid with Christ in God."—
Col. iii. 3.

Rejoice, believer in the Lord,
  Who makes your cause His own;
The hope that's built upon His word
  Can ne'er be overthrown.

Though many foes beset your road,
  And feeble is your arm,
Your life is hid with Christ in God,
  Beyond the reach of harm.

Weak as you are, you shall not faint,
  Or fainting shall not die;
Jesus, the strength of every saint,
  Shall aid you from on high.

Though sometimes unperceived by sense,
  Faith sees Him always near,
A guide, a glory, a defence;
  Then what have you to fear?

As surely as He overcame
And triumph'd once for you,
So surely you that love His name
Shall triumph in Him too.

NEWTON.

"Yield yourselves unto God."—Rom. vi. 17.

PEACE has unveil'd her smiling face
And woos thy soul to her embrace;
Enjoy'd with ease if thou refrain
From selfish love, else sought in vain;
She dwells with all who Truth prefer,
But seeks not them who seek not her.

Yield to the Lord with simple heart
All that thou hast, and all thou art;
Renounce all strength but strength divine;
And peace shall be for ever thine:
Lo, this the path which I have trod,
My path, till I go home to God.

COWPER, *from* GUYON.

"I will not go out free."—Exodus xxi. 5, 6.

I LOVE, I love my Master,
  I will not go out free;
For He is my Redeemer,
  He paid the price for me.

I would not leave His service,
  It is so sweet and blest;
And in the weariest moments
  He gives the truest rest.

I would not halve my service,
  His only it must be;
His only—who so loved me,
  And gave Himself for me.

My Master shed His life-blood
  My vassal life to win,
And save me from the bondage
  Of tyrant self and sin.

He chose me for His service,
And gave me power to choose
That blessed, perfect freedom,
Which I shall never lose.

For He has met my longing
With words of golden tone,
That I "shall serve for ever"
Himself, Himself alone.

Rejoicing and adoring,
Henceforth my song shall be,—
"I love, I love my Master,
I will not go out free!"

MISS F. R. HAVERGAL.

From "Hymns of Consecration and Faith," by permission.

"Doth He thank that servant?"—Luke xvii. 7-9.

The day's long work is done, the west is red,
The plough stands still, the gather'd sheep are fed;
And I, the Master's servant, turn and come,
From furrow'd field and pastoral upland, home;
Home, 'neath the vesper star to still repose,
Home, on the sounds of day the door to close,
Home, to the twilight hour of peace and prayer,
Home, but a servant still, to meet my Master there.

The quiet house is His, and therefore mine,
Who also am His own by right divine;
Nor place nor time his faithful bondmen claim,
Save for His will and work, and in His name.

Lord Jesus Christ, in chamber as in field
I live to Thee, to Thee my soul I yield;
And now the hands that plough'd for Thee, and fed,
Thy evening meal must dress, Thy table spread:—
'Tis done, 'tis ready; deign to sit and eat;
I gird myself, and serve Thee, as is meet.

* * *

What is His fare? Alas, no sumptuous board
Lies heap'd with angels' bread to greet my Lord;
Here's nought for banquet but myself, my soul,
Meekly anew presented, part and whole.

He does not thank His bondman. Do I praise
My hand, my foot, because it still obeys,
Attends the head's commandment, and exists
Only to work its thoughts, and labour as it lists?

* * * * *

Awhile He eats; He condescends to see
Some of the travail of His soul in me;
Then rises, bids me take a brother's chair,
And is Himself the bread, and feeds me there.

Sweet is the night that follows on such meal,
And happy slumbers o'er the servant steal;
Till, when the orient glows, he wakes amain,
And hies him to the field and fold again.

H. C. G. M.
October, 1887

"What has been chiefly on my mind lately has been how little and how poorly we ask and seek after the help and blessing we need, for and in everything.

"I have been much helped by this suggestion—to give in our relation to others, (children, servants, poor neighbours,) to give what we receive, and *only* what we receive; not to act from the surface of our minds, but from their deep places; not from impulse, but from a supply to be sought and obtained of true sap from the true Vine. The same words, the same discipline, are different in their effects as they are the fruit of the natural heart, or that of the heart united to Christ. We must pause, not only to ask for blessing on what we do, but to come empty and receive from Him, to 'get orders,' and this especially in the beginning of the day; to take our vessels to be filled with what God is ready to give—even love, patience, gentleness, courage, and firmness."

MRS. JOHNSTON (*ob.* 1852), daughter of the late Sir T. FOWELL BUXTON.

From an unpublished Memoir, by kind permission.

Woodfall & Kinder, Printers, 70 to 76, Long Acre, W.C.

www.ingramcontent.com/pod-product-compliance
Lightning Source LLC
Chambersburg PA
CBHW020241170426
43202CB00008B/174

* 9 7 8 3 3 3 7 3 3 6 7 9 0 *